FEMINIST DRAMA

DEFINITION & CRITICAL ANALYSIS

JANET BROWN

THE SCARECROW PRESS, INC.
METUCHEN, N.J., & LONDON
1979

Library of Congress Cataloging in Publication Data

Brown, Janet, 1952-
  Feminist drama.

    Bibliography: p.
    Includes index.
    1. American drama--20th century--History and
criticism. 2. Feminism in literature. 3. Women
dramatists, American--Biography. I. Title.
PS338.W6B7   812'.5'4093   79-22382
ISBN 0-8108-1267-3

To Sandy Nickel, who encouraged me to write on this topic and who forced me to re-think it many times; to Carla Waal, my advisor, who supported me through the process of committees and revisions with great kindness; and to my mother, Patricia Brown, who would have preferred a novel.

ACKNOWLEDGMENTS

I thank Dolores Walker of the Westbeth Playwrights' Feminist Collective, Dinah Leavitt of the Boulder Feminist Theatre, Ada McAllister of the Rhode Island Feminist Theatre, Judy Sarver of the B & O, Cynthia A. Ferguson and other members of Circle of the Witch for sending materials and for sharing their time and experiences with me.

CONTENTS

CHAPTER 1

INTRODUCTION

A few years ago an upsurge of feminist activity in the United States led to the formation of feminist theatre groups in several cities. Reading about these groups, I became interested in the idea of feminist drama and how one might determine what is feminist about a play. Of course, these theatre groups were and are producing what they call feminist drama. But I felt that other plays might also qualify as feminist drama, although their authors might not be politically active feminists. Such drama might, nevertheless, express feminist thinking in what Kenneth Burke would call its "rhetorical motive."

Burke's theory that all literature has a rhetorical or persuasive motive attracted me to his writings. Unlike many other literary critics, Burke does not focus on the distinction between a work's artistic merit and its message. Rather, the artistry of a work, in his view, is its rhetorical strategy, its method of delivering a message. Feminism, like Burkean theory, has attempted to link art with life, and literature with politics. Like other social movements, the feminist movement has proclaimed that "the personal is political." Therefore, it seems particularly appropriate to employ a Burkean methodology in determining whether a play is feminist in its rhetorical motive.

In order to make this determination, however, one must first have at least a working definition of feminism. Although the feminist movement has inspired a mass of printed matter in the past ten years, relatively little of this is ideological or theoretical. From the attempts that have been made in the direction of feminist ideology, as well as from broad reading in other feminist literature, I have derived the concept of a feminist impulse. This feminist impulse is expressed dramatically in woman's struggle for autonomy against an oppressive, sexist society. When woman's struggle for autonomy is a play's central rhetorical motive, that play can be considered a feminist drama.

1

A Burkean methodology can be employed, then, to examine a play's rhetorical motive, and to compare this motive
with my definition of the feminist impulse. Such a process
can serve, not simply to categorize plays as feminist or otherwise, but to elucidate what their rhetorical motives are,
to clarify what is feminist about certain plays, and to refine
the definition of the feminist impulse posited here. I have
selected five plays from the wealth of contemporary American
drama as a demonstration of this method of analysis. Four
of these plays have the feminist impulse as their rhetorical
motive. One deals with related concerns, and might popularly be considered a feminist play, but does not have the feminist impulse as its rhetorical motive. "Rhetorical motive"
is used here in Burke's sense. Besides the five plays examined in depth I have also analyzed the rhetorical strate-
gies--using the term "rhetorical" here in its more general
sense--of a selection of plays by feminist theatre groups. In
all of these analyses, I have employed a Burkean methodology
to examine the feminist impulse as a rhetorical motive in
drama.

Burkean Methodology

        At the root of Burke's theory of literary form is the
idea that a rhetorical or persuasive motive inspires the symbolic act which is literature. Literature is a purposeful response, a strategy for responding to some human situation.
It is always purposely designed to meet this situation:

> Critical and imaginative works are answers to
> questions posed by the situations in which they
> arose. They are not merely answers, they are
> strategic answers, stylized answers. ... So I
> should propose an initial working distinction be-
> tween "strategies" and "situations" whereby we think
> of poetry (I here use the term to include any work
> of critical or imaginative cast) as the adopting of
> various strategies for the encompassing of situa-
> tions. These strategies size up situations, name
> their structure and outstanding ingredients, and
> name them in a way that contains an attitude to-
> wards them. 1

This naming is the work itself: a symbolic act. "We might
sum all this up by saying that poetry, or any verbal act, is
to be considered as 'symbolic action.' "2

The author, according to Burke, can never be completely conscious of all the interrelationships that express a
work's attitude while he or she is still in the act of creating
it.   When the work is complete, however, a reader may examine the work for "associational clusters" that will reveal
the play's pattern of symbolic action, and therefore its rhetorical motive. These associational clusters are the implied
equations in a work.   One may, by examining a work, "find
what goes with what in these clusters--what kinds of acts and
images and personalities and situations go with the author's
notions of heroism, villainy, consolation, despair, etc. "3   By
examining associational clusters, the critic "may disclose by
objective citation the structure of motivation operating here.
There is no need to 'supply' motives. The interrelationships
themselves are his [/her] motives. For they are his [/her]
situations; and situation is but another word for motives. "4
This type of inspection is "statistical" in Burkean terms because it "counts up" associations and then attempts to generalize about the pattern of symbolic action on the basis of
these associations.   The generalizations should reveal what
is thematically related or thematically opposed, and thus the
structure of symbolic action should become apparent.   These
associations may occur among characters, actions, events,
objects, and images.   And they may occur on one of three
levels: the abstract, the personal, and the sensory or bio-
logical.   The same attitude may be expressed in different
terms on all three of these levels.   All of the elements in a
cluster "equal" one another.   Each cluster can be represented
or identified by one of its elements on any of the three levels.
Burke illustrates the concept of clusters with a play, Clifford
Odets' Golden Boy.   This play, he says, is formed around
the symbol of the violin, the other forming around the symbol of the prize-fight.   These two clusters form the play's
central opposition.

As important to Burke's system as the quantity and
kind of associations is their placement in the work.   According to Burke, "we should watch for 'critical points' within
the work, as well as at beginnings and endings.   There are
often 'watershed moments, ' changes of slope, where some
new quality enters. "5   Such a moment is often exhibited by
a shift in the pattern of associations at some critical point.

In A Grammar of Motives, written after The Philosophy of Literary Form from which the above terms are drawn,
Burke suggests another set of terms with which to discuss
the pattern of symbolic action.   This set, unlike the earlier

one, is applicable to life as easily as to literature. It is
Burke's well-known pentad: Agent, Act, Agency, Scene, and
Purpose. Once again his intent is to reveal the rhetorical
motive behind an event, this time by analyzing the relationship among these five elements.

Burke emphasizes that these relationships, or "ratios,"
serve to link the five parts so that each is interdependent on
the others. Focusing on the ratio between any two of these
parts reveals the way in which the two interrelate "synec-
dochically." For instance, acts must be in keeping with the
scene in which they occur; that is, they must be implicit
within that scene itself. Similarly, scene defines the agent
who must arise from such a scene, and agent and act help
to define scene.

Remember that all works contain all five elements
and ten ratios. Burke is suggesting only that by focusing
on one element or ratio, by selecting it as significant, one
can gain a specific insight about the work. Expanding on
this idea, Burke adds that different philosophic schools "fea-
ture" different terms from the pentad. That is:

> Dramatistically, the different philosophic schools
> are to be distinguished by the fact that each school
> features a different one of the five terms, in de-
> veloping a vocabulary designed to allow this one
> term full expression (as regards its resources and
> its temptations) with the other terms being com-
> paratively slighted or being placed in the perspec-
> tive of the featured term. [6]

Burke develops the relationship between the terms of
the pentad and the philosophic schools in detail. But the
concept of philosophic schools is chiefly useful to this study
simply in clarifying the significance of each term of the pentad. The philosophies associated with each term follow:

> For the featuring of scene, the corresponding
> philosophic terminology is materialism.
> For the featuring of agent, the corresponding
> terminology is idealism.
> For the featuring of agency, the corresponding
> terminology is pragmatism.
> For the featuring of purpose, the corresponding
> terminology is mysticism.
> For the featuring of act, the corresponding ter-
> minology is realism. [7]

The terms of the pentad combine to form a drama, or action, which is a paradigm of history. The initial state in this drama is an ordered hierarchy. Then an agent disobeys this hierarchy "for men [human beings] are by nature divided: capable of rising, hence of falling; of accepting, consenting, obeying--hence of rejecting, dissenting, disobeying."[8] Having disobeyed, the agent experiences Guilt, and experiencing Guilt, dreams of salvation, of a more perfect order than the present one. "And thus, perversely goaded by the spirit of hierarchy, moved by the impious dream of a mythic new Order--inspired with a new purpose, drawn anew by desire--they are moved to act--moved, ingenious men [human beings] ('inventors of the negative') to rise up and cry No to the existing order--and prophesy the coming of the new."[9]

Redemption, however, requires a Redeemer, a Victim. If the drama ends in Victimage, a scapegoat is sacrificed for the sake of the new order. If the end is Mortification, in the order of perfect love, the agent may sacrifice himself or herself for the sake of the new order. Such a drama is a struggle for perfection. Though it is grounded in Guilt, needing Redemption, requiring a Redeemer-Victim, "Yet it must not be forgotten that rhetoric, though in the order of killing, is also in the order of love. For it includes communication; and 'communication' is the most generalized statement of the principle of 'love.'"[10]

The pentad operates as a means of analyzing the pattern of symbolic action. One first determines what the five terms are in a particular work or event, and then which of the relationships, or ratios, between the terms is the most revealing of the pattern of symbolic action.

A play's rhetorical motive can be identified by employing Burke's method, and its pattern of symbolic action can be evaluated. A play, according to Burke, is a strategy for encompassing a situation. Therefore, it can be evaluated by how successfully it encompasses that situation. That is, to the degree that a play's rhetorical strategy addresses the complexities of its situation, the play is rhetorically successful. In evaluating a play with a feminist rhetorical motive, the critic considers whether the play's strategies are as rhetorically sophisticated as necessary to encompass the situation of woman in a sexist society. A play that shows this degree of rhetorical sophistication can be considered a successful feminist drama.

Because of its focus on rhetorical motive, Burkean methodology seems especially appropriate to the analysis of the feminist impulse. Burke, in describing his approach to analysis, says, "It assumes that a poem's structure is to be described most accurately by thinking always of the poem's function. It assumes that the poem is designed to 'do something' for the poet and his [/her] readers, and that we can make the most relevant observations about its design by considering the poem as the embodiment of this act."[11]

Burke's concern with the function of art makes his method highly appropriate to the study of feminist drama. However, the pattern of symbolic action which he describes conflicts directly with Mary Daly's concept of a feminist symbolism outlined in her philosophical work, Beyond God the Father. [12] Daly would agree with Burke that the symbolic pattern of an unjust society absolved by the sacrifice of a scapegoat has permeated history and literature and, more importantly to Daly, religion as well. This very pattern, however, provides sexist society with its justification and encourages the continuance of women's oppression in Daly's view.

Daly finds the dominant Judeo-Christian tradition founded upon guilt and therefore necessitating scapegoats to expiate this guilt. In the myth of the garden of Eden, Eve is made the original scapegoat for humanity's guilt. The early Church fathers condemned women as entirely sexual and sinful, questioning whether they had souls. In the Middle Ages, women were burned as witches to purge the community of evil. Throughout history, Daly maintains, women have been scapegoats, suffering for the guilt created by patriarchal religion.

Theoretically, Jesus Christ is Christianity's scapegoat, sacrificed for the sins of all. But society does not respond to this myth by imitating Christ's behavior; instead his sacrifice produces guilt and therefore a further need for scapegoats to expiate this guilt. Women have traditionally filled this need, according to Daly, imitating Christ's suffering but unable to share in his role as spiritually powerful priest because of their gender.

The true Second Coming, according to Daly, will be the feminist movement's creation of a new consciousness. This new consciousness will be created by women who dare to face "non-being" in the fact of their own "non-existence" in society--society's failure to recognize their full humanity. The confrontation with non-being is a transforming experience, a communal, sororal experience of the sacred. The sacred is experienced not as a patriarchal god or as the society's scapegoat, but as an ongoing process: in Daly's term, as God the Verb.

In this new consciousness, male and female characteristics as well as good and evil will be recognized as components of every individual. Because there will be no need to expiate guilt over a suffering god, and no assumption that evil can be isolated in certain individuals or classes of society, there will be no need for scapegoats.

Daly recognizes, however, that this Second Coming is in the present and in the future. The pattern of symbolic action described by Burke has permeated history and dominates even feminist literature and drama today. The most recent feminist drama and that which is most in touch with the evolution of feminist philosophy is only beginning to move beyond the isolated, sacrificial hero to a pattern in which there are many protagonists and no scapegoats. Both the dominant pattern in which a single agent struggles for her autonomy and the emerging pattern described by Daly will be observed and analyzed in the course of this work.

Burke's primary value to the following chapters is his focus on rhetorical motive. Because Burke does not make the Aristotelian distinction between mimetic and didactic art, his method avoids some of the difficulties encountered by critics employing the mimetic/didactic distinction.

Review of Dramatic and Literary Criticism

Among the critics who have struggled with the definition of didactic drama are Sam Smiley in The Drama of Attack,[13] Gerald Rabkin in The Drama of Commitment,[14] and Michael W. Kaufman in "The Delicate World of Reprobation."[15] Sam Smiley, analyzing social drama of the thirties, employs Aristotle's definitions of the rhetorical as well as of the poetic. He sees these social dramas as both rhetorical (that is, persuasive) and poetic (that is, beautiful). A play is didactic to the degree that thought, rather than plot or character, is the dominant part: "One may learn from any drama, but only didactic drama is meant primarily as an instrument of instruction or persuasion."[16] The mimetic drama permits learning; the didactic drama compels it.

8 Feminist Drama

The practical difficulty of defining any specific play in terms of these polarities is apparent in Smiley's conclusions. All of the plays so intelligently analyzed naturally turn out to be a mixture of both didacticism and mimesis, with perhaps a special emphasis on one or the other. Burke's theory, that all communication including the most purely artistic is rhetorical because it attempts to persuade the audience of its particular vision of life, obviates the need for this distinction.

Gerald Rabkin, in Drama of Commitment, attempts to relate literature to life by focusing upon the political and moral stance of social playwrights of the thirties, that is, upon their degree of "committedness." He succeeds in relating biography to literary production, but not in confirming or denying the hypothesis that degree or kind of committedness affects the aesthetic result. Instead, he concludes that "neither sound ideology nor sound theology can fill the void of esthetic deficiency."[17] On the other hand, audiences should not "commit the contrary heresy of damning those works whose commitments we reject."[18] Rabkin's own attachment to the distinction between "ideology" and "esthetics" limits his conclusions. By employing a Burkean methodology, he might have concentrated instead on the rhetorical strategy the writers employed as an integration of both.

Michael W. Kaufman, in an article on black revolutionary theatre, calls this drama rhetorical because the authors define the world on their own terms, and because their drama is "consciously intended to excite an audience to act decisively and to transform their lives and the society that oppresses them."[19] In a Burkean methodology, all literature fulfills the first requirement of attempting to define the world. The second requirement, that the audience is asked to act in the world outside of the theatre, is a more distinctive factor. Kaufman points out one characteristic of many of the plays he examines, an "open-endedness" even to the point of finishing a play in the middle of a sentence. The effect, according to Kaufman, is to bring the audience "only to the threshold of fulfillment," to impel them to revolutionary action.[20]

This description recalls Burke's historical cycle. In the cycle, the existing order is perceived as unjust by an agent who dreams of a new and more perfect order. Guilt at rejecting the existing order impels the agent to attempt the establishment of a new and more perfect order. A black

revolutionary drama which ended on "the threshold of fulfillment" might function as the first step in this cycle, the ne-
gation of the existing order impelling the audience toward
the enactment of the entire cycle.

Smiley, Rabkin, and Kaufman all demonstrate the
problems of examining didactic drama either in the light of
Aristotelian theory or without employing any stated methodology.   Burkean methodology, by assuming a rhetorical motive in all literature, avoids some of the problems confronted
by other critical methods.

By assuming such a rhetorical motive, this methodology lends itself with special appropriateness to feminist
criticism.   Feminism, like Burkean methodology, has re-
fused to separate art from life or literature from politics.
Instead, by analyzing the sexual images and stereotypes in
literature, by relating history and biography to literature,
by examining the relation of literary structure to content, or
by analyzing rhetorical strategies of the feminist movement
itself, feminist criticism has always attempted to integrate
art and life.   With the exception of the unpublished disserta-
tions by Hope and Zastrow described below, however, feminist criticism has not attempted to apply Burke's theories
directly in developing a methodology.   Nor has it attempted
to define the feminist impulse in literature, as this study
will do.

One type of feminist literary criticism analyzes images and stereotypes of women in literature, usually literature written by men.   Perhaps the most notorious instance
of this type is Kate Millett's Sexual Politics, in which she
attacks the sexist stereotyping of Mailer, Miller, and Genet. [21]
Perhaps the earliest and certainly one of the best examples
of this type of criticism is The Second Sex by Simone de
Beauvoir. [22]   In Part III of her encyclopedic work, de Beauvoir examines woman as "other," appearing in the works of
Montherlant, D. H. Lawrence, Claudel, Breton, and Stend-
hal.   She employs close linguistic analysis in demonstrating
that female characters are portrayed as both less than and
more than human.

Following de Beauvoir, many critics have examined
the social stereotypes in literature.   Exemplifying this type
of criticism are Up Against the Wall, Mother, [23] an anthology divided according to the stereotypical image of women
presented in each section's readings; American Sisterhood by

Wendy Martin, [24] which examines the myth of the American
heroine as Eve cursed for eating the apple of experience;
and Roger's The Troublesome Helpmate, [25] which examines
misogyny in Western literature.

Historical and biographical criticism is a second kind
of feminist critique exemplified by Suzanne Juhasz's Naked
and Fiery Forms, a study of twentieth-century poetry by
major women authors. [26] Juhasz defines herself as a feminist critic because of her recognition of the effect of society
upon the work of women writers. She believes that women
poets in our society are in a "double bind." Because society perceives "poet" as a male role, "woman" and "poet"
become contradictory identities. It is out of the tension between these identities that women's poetry arises. Juhasz
finds a recurring attempt on the part of these poets to grow
beyond the imitation of male writers and to develop a female
poetry of engagement and integration, less abstract and less
prone to generalization than that of men. Juhasz indicates
at first that this is a pattern of development she has observed in successful women writers. But later she con-
demns even such presumably successful women writers as
the poet Marianne Moore, if their writings do not follow this
pattern. As a result, confusion arises in this book. It is
never clear whether the pattern of development Juhasz describes is intended to be descriptive or prescriptive.

Ellen Moers offers historical feminist criticism of
another kind in Literary Women. [27] Moers focuses on nine-
teenth-century women writers as a new phenomenon of this
time, and detects a shared literary tradition of women authors reading and responding to one another. The book also
examines the possibility of recurrent imagery which may be
unique to women writers. This possibility, she admits, is
hard to substantiate in any concrete way.

An unpublished dissertation by Sylvia Virginia Horning
Zastrow examines the structure of selected plays by American women playwrights in the years 1920-1970. [28] She attempts to find adaptation of structure to content, unique to
the work of women playwrights. She fails to find such an
adaptation in most of the plays she examines, and believes
that the plays ultimately fail for this reason. Like Smiley,
Zastrow incorporates an essentially Aristotelian approach,
distinguishing didacticism from mimesis, but she also incorporates Francis Fergusson's analysis of the relationship between structure and purpose. Her discussion of playwrights'

purposes stems from Burke's theory and the analysis of
Burke's work by his critics.   The work is organized historically, focusing on twentieth-century women writers who
have won or been nominated for Broadway or off-Broadway
awards, beginning with Rachel Crothers and ending with Megan Terry.   Although Zastrow employs Burke, she does so
only peripherally, and not for purposes of defining and analyzing the feminist impulse as will be attempted in this work.
This selection represents only a small sample of the current
feminist literary and dramatic criticism.

Review of Rhetorical Criticism

        A related field also relevant to this study is that of
rhetorical criticism.   Karlyn Kohrs Campbell has examined
the rhetoric of women's liberation and maintains that, because women's liberation as a movement involves a state of
mind rather than politics in the usual sense, its rhetoric
may be distinct from movement rhetoric both in substance
and in style. [29]   Substantively, it involves a deeper societal
change than other movements.   The very role of rhetor,
because it is an active one, violates the female role according to Campbell.   The very existence of feminist rhetoric attacks the most fundamental values of the culture.   Therefore,
although feminist rhetoric may be moderate in form, it is
invariably radical in substance.

        Stylistically, she finds feminist rhetoric unique in its
lack of leaders and rhetors, in its existence as a process
of discovering a new identity rather than as a policy, in its
distinctness from psychoanalysis because the personal dis-
coveries of women are applied at a social structure level,
and in that its rhetoric is characterized by non-adjustive
strategies designed to show unconscious sexism.

        Other feminist rhetorical criticism includes an article
by Marie J. Rosenwasser delineating the phases of feminist
rhetoric according to the phases of movement rhetoric, con-
cluding that the movement is and probably will remain in the
third phase of conversion and change since progress toward
the phases of solidification and success would require sweep-
ing change in social attitudes. [30]

        Diane S. Hope has completed an unpublished disserta-
tion in which she examines feminist political rhetoric for a
"drama of rebirth" which she sees appearing as an image in

this type of rhetoric.[31] She employs radical feminism as a
case study in evaluating three methodological assumptions
about movement rhetoric to be used in defining the rhetorical
movement. These assumptions are, first, that rhetorical
movements begin when changes in the rhetorical scene create rhetorical crisis for alienated groups; second, that each
rhetorical movement articulates a specific "drama of conflict" which reconstructs reality for its participants through
plot, motive, and characters; and third, that the rhetorical
style of a movement is largely determined by the symbolic
drama as the legitimate response to dramatic tensions between conflicting characters.

     Hope's study of the radical feminist movement demon-
strates a symbolic "drama" in its rhetoric, a pattern of
death and rebirth which has as its components: a) Isolation
of participants through redefinition. Women defined as a
lower caste. b) Sharing of previously unshared cultural secrets through feminist literature and consciousness-raising
groups. c) Victimization and symbolic death of the traditional woman as rebirth occurs through acceptance of movement reality.

     Although this "drama" centers on a "kill," man is
not the victim.

> Contrary to some analyses of the radical feminist
> movement the emergent victim is not men, although
> men are clearly seen as the enemy. The real
> victim is "traditional womanhood" or as another
> feminist writes, "the enemy ... in your head."
> The victim is traditional woman, for it is the
> "male-identified woman" who was condemned to
> acquiesce in her own oppression, who was social-
> ized by the male definition of her sexual identity,
> and identified as an appendage to man. Until this
> socialized identity was killed off, the new woman
> could not be born.[32]

This "plot" is of interest because it translates movement
rhetoric into dramatistic terms, but also because of its emphasis on internal conflict, on the death and rebirth of the
woman herself as subject instead of object.

> Discussion and persuasion surrounding the feminist
> position ... centers on the unique rhetorical strat-
> egy of radical feminism; to redefine the personal

> and psychological as political.... The purpose of
> the rhetoric is simple--woman must be made sub-
> ject to her self.[33]

Or, in other words, woman must become autonomous. Hope's
work is of special concern to this study because it employs
a Burkean methodology in examining feminist rhetoric.

Hope has also written a comparison of the rhetoric
of the black movement and that of the women's liberation
movement.[34] Both movements share the rhetorical task of
redefinition of self. But there are three significant rhetorical differences between them. First, "metaphorical use suggests that the black movement assumes the dominant white
culture's value of sexism; the women's movement attempts to
overcome white racism." Secondly, "black rhetors can assume a pre-existing audience; feminist rhetors must first
create the group and consequently an audience." Finally,
"black rhetoric generates a counter-movement; feminist rhetoric generates only backlash, public silence, and private
ridicule."[35]

A survey of existing feminist criticism--rhetorical,
dramatic, and literary--reveals no attempt to define what
is feminist about certain works of literature. Attempts have
been made to define what is unique in feminist rhetoric, but
these have not extended to the use of literature as material
for analysis. On the other hand, feminist criticism consistently shows a concern with the integration of art and life
which should make it peculiarly adapted to application of a
Burkean methodology.

Defining the Feminist Impulse

In order to ascertain what is feminist about certain
plays, a feminist impulse must first be defined which would
serve as Burke's "rhetorical motive" and which would be the
common link among feminist plays. Simone de Beauvoir, in
The Second Sex, points out that in a male-defined culture,
"humanity is male and man defines woman not in herself,
but as relative to him; she is not regarded as an autonomous
being." This is because "woman has always been man's
dependent, if not his slave; the two sexes have never shared
the world in equality."[36] There are two essential parts to
this definition: one, that women as a group are powerless
subordinates of men; the other, that woman as an individual
is not an autonomous being.

The demand for woman's autonomy figures frequently in definitions of feminism. Aileen S. Kraditor, in her introduction to Up from the Pedestal, describes the "something" which the feminist writings she has anthologized have in common:

> This fundamental something can perhaps be designated by the term "autonomy." Whether a feminist's demand has been for all the rights men have had, or for some but not all of the rights men have had, or for certain rights that men have not had, the grievance behind the demand has always seemed to be that women have been regarded not as people but as female relatives of people. And the feminists' desire has, consequently, been for women to be recognized, in the economic, political, and/or social realms, as individuals in their own right.[37]

Gerda Lerner, in The Female Experience, uses remarkably similar terms:

> This process of creating feminist consciousness has something, but by no means everything to do with the quest for women's rights, equality, and justice--it has a great deal to do with the search for autonomy.... Autonomy means moving out from a world in which one is born to marginality, to a past without meaning, and a future determined by others--into a world in which one acts and chooses, aware of a meaningful past and free to shape one's future.[38]

Lerner goes on, however, to outline phases or variations in the feminist ideology. The initial stage in attaining a feminist consciousness, Lerner says, is a woman's coming to self-consciousness, becoming aware of a distortion or a wrong in her own societal status as woman. At this point she sees men as the enemy.

The second step questions tradition, and tentatively moves in new directions. The third step is a reaching out for others, a search for sisterhood, often involving organized groups of women. Arising out of this quest for union is the fourth step, feminist consciousness, defined as the search for autonomy.

Veronica Geng remarks that women have often phrased their protest so that it seems that vague "forces" and "societal roles" are to blame for their situation. Betty Friedan, for instance, in The Feminine Mystique,

> acknowledged de Beauvoir's "insights into French women," but chose to present American women with a "problem that has no name," or a problem that has a not very good name--"feminine mystique"--instead of a problem with the vivid and particular name that de Beauvoir had given it: the historic domination of women by men. [39]

But it is because of this domination, this denial of power to women, that the feminist impulse is a radical one, inspiring a rhetoric of confrontation. In Burkean terms, feminists have said "no" to the unjust order and have challenged existing structures of reality with a new vision: a vision of woman as autonomous, as fully human.

The definition of the feminist impulse to be employed in this work will be: the impulse towards woman's autonomy in a society in which women, as a group, are powerless. Phrasing this definition in Burke's terms, a feminist drama is one on which the agent is a woman, her purpose autonomy, and her scene a society in which women are powerless. Such a society is the "unjust socio-sexual hierarchy" Burke has described in analyzing Shakespeare's Venus and Adonis:

> To see such developments as dominantly sexual is indeed to be sex-ridden. Rather, one should scrutinize them for certain principles of courtship, a social manifestation, which by the same token figures a hierarchic motive. The vocabularies of social and sexual courtship are so readily interchangeable, not because one is a mere "substitute" for the other, but because sexual courtship is intrinsically fused with the motives of social hierarchy. [40]

The socio-sexual hierarchy is the scene in a feminist drama.

The two significant elements to consider in determining whether a play is feminist by this method are agent and scene. Examination of a play's clusters of associations will reveal the interrelationships in the play, and how the society

represented in the play is structured. Examination of a
play's pattern of symbolic action will reveal who the agent
is, and what the agent's purpose is in following the pattern
of action.   Thus, analysis of the associational clusters will
reveal the play's socio-sexual hierarchy; analysis of the pattern of symbolic action will reveal the agent and her purpose.
If the agent is a woman, her purpose autonomy, and the
scene an unjust socio-sexual hierarchy, the play is a feminist drama.

        A significant ratio, then, would be the agent:scene
ratio.   Burke, explaining the "synecdochic" relation, or
ratio between agent and scene, indicates that each is implicit in the other.   That is, in this instance, an unjust socio-
sexual hierarchy results in women demanding autonomy.   Or,
in other words, women demanding autonomy are implicit
within such an unjust hierarchy.   Without such a scene, the
agent would not exist.   Similarly, without members of a
group denied power and therefore demanding autonomy, the
scene would not be an unjust socio-sexual hierarchy.

        The analysis of these two elements, agent and scene,
will indicate whether a play is a feminist drama.   Further,
to the degree that scene or agent is the element emphasized,
the play's affinity to a particular school of philosophy will
be indicated.   Recall that the corresponding philosophic term
for the featuring of agent is idealism, and for the featuring
of scene, materialism.   It then follows that, to the extent
that the agent's achievement of autonomy is featured, the
play will be idealistic.   To the extent that the scene, the
unjust socio-sexual hierarchy, is featured, the play will be
materialistic.   According to Burke, materialism and idealism
are opposites, the one reducing all that exists to matter,
the other idealizing what is material and thus transforming
it into spirit or symbol.

        Materialism, because it supposes a material or nat-
ural cause to everything, is allied with determinism, or the
idea that whatever happens is dictated by the environment,
out of the control of the individual.   Idealism posits the opposite, a theory which "seeks the explanation, or ultimate
raison d'être, of the cosmic evolution in the realization of
reason, self-consciousness, or spirit. "   These two forces
can be observed in conflict in the feminist drama.   To the
extent that agent or scene dominates, the play is idealistic
or materialistic in its philosophic conclusions.

If it is idealistic, the individual agent will succeed in asserting her autonomy either by spiritually transcending the unjust hierarchy or by sacrificing herself for a new and more
perfect order in an act of mortification. If the play is materialistic, the environment, the unjust hierarchy, will prevail. The agent will not achieve autonomy, but will be sacrificed to the existing order. But whether the play's conclusion is idealistic or materialistic, if the play features as
its agent a woman seeking autonomy in an unjust socio-sexual hierarchy, it can be considered a feminist drama.

Play Selection

        In the present work six contemporary American
plays chosen from wide reading in this area will be examined. Also included is a selection of the work written by
feminist theatre groups in the past few years. The plays
examined at length were chosen because they demonstrate
the range and limits of the expression of the feminist rhetorical impulse. The plays vary in style, subject, and conclusions.

        The Bed Was Full is a farcical presentation of a
woman's evasion of her society's attempts to force her to
play stereotypical, limited sexual roles.[41] It is non-realistic in style and deterministic in its conclusions. Its author,
Rosalyn Drexler, is often identified as a feminist playwright.
In the Boom Boom Room, in contrast, was written by a
man, David Rabe, and was critically regarded as simply an
individual story of a Philadelphia go-go dancer.[42] The play
expresses a feminist rhetorical motive, however, in its depiction of a socio-sexual hierarchy in the barroom society
of the play, and in its pattern of symbolic action, the agent's
struggle to assert her autonomy in this society. In the
Boom Boom Room develops its plot and characters in realistic style, in complete contrast to The Bed Was Full, but
shares that play's deterministic conclusions.

        Wine in the Wilderness, another serious, realistic
play, is optimistic in its conclusions.[43] Written by Alice
Childress, a black playwright, this play examines the black
woman's uniquely difficult struggle toward autonomy in opposition to the spectre of the "black matriarchy." Tina
Howe's Birth and After Birth is included as an example of
a play that is popularly identified as feminist drama, but
that does not have a feminist rhetorical motive.[44] This

play is a comical, non-realistic examination of the contemporary nuclear family.

   In the sixth chapter, several rhetorical strategies common to the work of feminist theatre groups are examined, with examples from five of these groups. A play employing each strategy is analyzed by the definition of feminist drama posited in this study. The analysis suggests the common strain shared by these plays and the plays written by individuals. It also reveals limitations of the definition employed here, and suggests the future evolution of feminist drama. Finally, For Colored Girls Who Have Considered Suicide / When the Rainbow Is Enuf by Ntozake Shange is analyzed in Chapter Seven.[45] This play, a series of poetic statements thematically united by black women's experiences, embodies the most recent trend in feminist drama.

   Feminist Drama: Definition and Critical Analysis is intended to suggest a definition of feminist drama and a method, based on Burkean theory, by which that definition can be applied. The method is then employed in the analysis of varied contemporary plays, including drama produced by feminist theatre groups and by individuals who are not a part of the feminist movement. The result should be the elucidation of the plays examined, as well as a test of the usefulness of the definition and methodology employed.

Notes

1. Kenneth Burke, The Philosophy of Literary Form (New York: Vintage Books, 1957-61), p. 3.

2. Ibid., p. 8.

3. Ibid., p. 18.

4. Ibid.

5. Ibid., p. 66.

6. Kenneth Burke, A Grammar of Motives and a Rhetoric of Motives (Cleveland: World Publishing Co., 1972), p. 127.

7. Ibid., p. 128.

8. Leland Griffin, "A Dramatistic Theory of the Rhetoric
    of Movements" in Critical Responses to Kenneth
    Burke, ed. William H. Rueckert (Minneapolis: Uni-
    versity of Minnesota Press, 1969), pp. 457-458.

9. Ibid., p. 460.

10. Ibid., p. 461.

11. Burke, Philosophy of Literary Form, p. 75.

12. Mary Daly, Beyond God the Father (Boston: Beacon
    Press, 1973).

13. Sam Smiley, The Drama of Attack (Columbia: Univer-
    sity of Missouri Press, 1972).

14. Gerald Rabkin, Drama and Commitment (Bloomington:
    Indiana University Press, 1964).

15. Michael W. Kaufman, "The Delicate World of Reproba-
    tion," Educational Theatre Journal 23 (December
    1971): 446-459.

16. Smiley, p. 6.

17. Rabkin, p. 295.

18. Ibid.

19. Kaufman, p. 449.

20. Ibid., p. 453.

21. Kate Millett, Sexual Politics (Garden City, N. Y.:
    Doubleday, 1970).

22. Simone de Beauvoir, The Second Sex, trans. H. M.
    Parshely (New York: Alfred A. Knopf, 1970).

23. Elsie Adams and Mary Louise Briscoe, ed., Up Against
    the Wall, Mother (Encino, Cal.: Glencoe, 1971).

24. Wendy Martin, The American Sisterhood (New York:
    Harper & Row, 1972).

25. Katherine M. Rogers, The Troublesome Helpmate (Se-
    attle: University of Washington Press, 1966).

26.   Suzanne Juhasz, Naked and Fiery Forms (New York:
       Harper Colophon Books, 1976).

27.   Ellen Moers, Literary Women (New York: Doubleday,
       1976).

28.   Sylvia Virginia Horning Zastrow, "The Structure of
       Selected Plays by American Women Playwrights:
       1920-1970" (Ph. D. dissertation, Northwestern Uni-
       versity, 1975).

29.   Karlyn Kohrs Campbell, "The Rhetoric of Women's Lib-
       eration: An Oxymoron," Quarterly Journal of Speech
       59 (February 1973): 74-86.

30.   Marie J. Rosenwasser, "Rhetoric and the Progress of
       the Women's Liberation Movement," Today's Speech
       10 (Summer 1972): 45-56.

31.   Diane S. Hope, "A Rhetorical Definition of Movements"
       (Ph. D. dissertation, State University of New York at
       Buffalo, 1975).

32.   Ibid., p. 160.

33.   Ibid., pp. 103-104.

34.   Diane S. Hope, "Redefinition of Self," Today's Speech
       23 (Winter 1975): 17-25.

35.   Ibid., p. 17.   Hope's point, that feminist rhetoric has
       generated no counter-movement, is more debatable
       now than it was in 1975 when this article was pub-
       lished.   Certainly, the ERA movement has encoun-
       tered a rhetoric of opposition which could be con-
       sidered an anti-feminist movement.

36.   Beauvoir, p. xviii.

37.   Aileen S. Kraditor, ed., Up from the Pedestal (Chicago:
       Quadrangle Books, 1968), p. 8.

38.   Gerda Lerner, The Female Experience (Indianapolis:
       Bobbs-Merrill Company, Inc., 1977), p. xxiv.

39.   Veronica Geng, "Requiem for the Women's Movement,"
       Harper's, November 1976, p. 51.

40. Kenneth Burke, A Grammar of Motives, p. 741.

41. Rosalyn Drexler, The Bed Was Full, The Line of Least Existence and Other Plays (New York: Random House, 1967).

42. David Rabe, In the Boom Boom Room (New York: Alfred A. Knopf, 1974).

43. Alice Childress, Wine in the Wilderness in Plays By and About Women, ed. Victoria Sullivan and James Hatch (New York: Random House, 1974).

44. Tina Howe, Birth and After Birth in The New Women's Theatre, ed. Honor Moore (New York: Random House, 1977).

45. Ntozake Shange, For Colored Girls Who Have Considered Suicide / When the Rainbow Is Enuf (New York: Macmillan Publishing Co., Inc., 1977).

CHAPTER 2

THE BED WAS FULL

Introduction

The Bed Was Full,* by Rosalyn Drexler, is a bed-room farce featuring the typical adulterous plot and stereo-typed characters. But one character in this farce, Kali, re-fuses to adopt a stereotypical role as the others do. The play's male characters, the "mounters" in the socio-sexual hierarchy, attempt to force Kali into a multitude of such roles. The pattern of symbolic action shows Kali's repeated evasions of their attempts, followed by her eventual submis-sion to the hierarchy.

Much of the play's humor arises from the pompous and irrational claims the characters make, from their sol-emn attempts to accomplish ridiculous ends, and from their stereotypical qualities as characters. The effect is not only to condemn the unjust socio-sexual hierarchy, but to poke fun at it as well. Although Kali sporadically resists being stereotyped by this ludicrous system, her own weakness and the threat of violence on which the system is based make her final defeat inevitable.

Biography

Rosalyn Drexler began her playwriting career as an escape from the confinement of her situation as a housewife:

> About 1960, 1961, I did it for spite. I was mar-ried and I couldn't get out very much and my daughter was young then. And I couldn't stand any-body knowing what I was doing. I had no privacy

---

*"The Bed Was Full," by Rosalyn Drexler in her The Line of Least Existence and Other Plays (New York: Random House, 1967). Quotes from this play reprinted by permission.

but when my kid went to school, I closed the door
and I said, Oh boy, this is my secret project and
I'm going to amuse myself. [1]

The result was her first play, Home Movies, later produced
off-Broadway by friends connected with the Judson Church
theatre. Drexler considers this environment to have been
unusually sympathetic to her work: "Maybe it has something
to do with economics. All artists together, men and women--
no money--you're working together and the big apple is pretty
far away."[2]

In 1964, Home Movies received an Obie award. Drexler has gone on to complete nine plays in all, and has had
an anthology of plays published, entitled The Line of Least
Existence. In 1973, she received a Rockefeller grant to
study playwriting abroad, and she is a member of the playwriting unit of the Actors' Studio.

Drexler's novels, like her plays, have characteristi-
cally shown an irreverent, punning humor. Critic Sara Sanborn describes this style:

> The raunchy and the ridiculous are Drexler's home
> territory--you feel that she spends a lot of time
> in all-night cafeterias. Her word-play is like
> sword-play--with rubber swords that still deliver
> a stinging slap.... She weaves a seamy web of
> parodies that cover the situation perfectly. Moving
> back and forth between the absurd and the every-
> day, Drexler puts both in their place--on the same
> plane. [3]

This humorous attitude imbues not only her plays and novels,
but her public presentation of herself as well.

Interviewed with other women playwrights by the staid
New York Times, Drexler distinguished herself as the only
respondent whose answers were completely flippant. Asked
where the woman playwrights are today, she replied:

> They are deployed about the city waiting to make
> their move. They have already learned how to
> take apart and put together their typewriters in a
> matter of minutes, and how to keep them clean and
> well lubricated. At a signal, which may be the
> clapping of one hand, all women playwrights will

> shoot the vapids and proceed to a secret rendez-
> vous where a hidden store of explosive topics are
> waiting to be used. With proper handling, each
> sentence will find its mark. [4]

This use of word play to make a satirical point is typical of
Drexler's early work. Critic Arthur Sainer notes, however,
that Drexler's most recent play, He Who Was She, is in a
different style:

> He Who Was She leaves the modern and concrete
> for the ancient and mythical. Its tone is lofty and
> even autumnal. Wounds are real and the murder
> of Queen Hatshepsut is very real. Drexler has
> gone back to pre-Biblical times to introduce the
> spectre of death and the transcendence of myth
> into her work. Ephemeral hijinks has given way,
> at least for the moment, to the eternal serious-
> ness of myth. [5]

The same, new interest in mythology is reflected in
a recent article by Drexler criticizing the current style of
dressing "androgynously":

> Diana is my household god: Diana of Ephesus,
> the multi-breasted goddess of the moon, of forests,
> of animals, of women in childbirth, whose temple
> was one of the seven wonders of the ancient world.
> I choose her fecund simplicity to protect me from
> the mutilations of androgyny and from a mock
> eroticism that begins and ends cold. [6]

This new seriousness and interest in women's mythic roots
parallels the progress of the feminist movement in recent
years. Just as the movement is beginning to emphasize
women's collective power and to be more direct in its demands, Drexler is beginning to adopt an approach that is
more affirmative of women and more comprehensive in its
treatment of serious topics.

The Bed Was Full, however, reflects Drexler's earlier, farcical style. Sainer describes it as having "a sense
of the old-fashioned, well-made play as well as of the par-
tially well-made Hollywood film, where things in the end are
patched up, where no real harm is done. What has been
done is solely to the spectator, not to the characters." [7]

Plot Summary

        The plot of The Bed Was Full is farcical and epi-
sodic. The play is described as taking place

>   on a ramp, hanging from a ramp, below a ramp,
>   and to the sides of a ramp. The top of the ramp
>   is an artist's studio.... Below is a middle-class
>   bedroom, bed light and all.... To the left is a
>   foyer with a parquet floor, like in a mansion. [8]

        The play opens with an artist, Dominick, and his
model, Kali. Discovering that they are both swingers, they
hold onto the edge of the platform flooring of their loft, and
swing down into the middle-class bedroom. This room belongs to Lewis and Vera, who are out. The Count appears
in the foyer. He enters the bedroom and tells Dominick that
he knew Kali first. Joel, a paranoid hired by Lewis to spy
on his wife, comes in and takes the Count captive, demanding that Dominick, whom he calls Lewis, pay him for the
capture. The Count, who is wearing a stiff shirtfront but
no shirt, mistakes Kali for his laundress and demands his
shirts. Vera and Lewis enter and Lewis accuses the Count
of "giving pleasure to someone who gives me pain.'" (p. 221)
Lewis decides against vengeance, however, in favor of a
whispered plan that no one understands. Everyone decides
that it means they should all get in bed.

        Joel returns and fights with his own image in the
mirror, eventually punching the mirror and cutting his hand
on the broken glass. Dominick paints him a bandage but decides it is art, and won't let Joel use it. Kali gives him
one of the Count's gloves to stop the bleeding, but the Count
fights him for the glove. Joel produces incriminating photo-
graphs of Vera and the Count. The Count attacks Lewis
with his cane, which causes Kali to fall in love with him.
Kali and Vera fight over the Count. Joel despairs of being
paid for his detective work, and Kali tells him not to jump.
He had not been contemplating suicide, but her remark inspires him to begin broadjumping. Joel jumps several
times, but no matter how far he jumps, Kali measures it
as fifteen feet.

        The Count turns out not to have been Vera's lover,
but Kali's. Dominick is at first jealous until Kali reveals
that the Count is Dominick's "secret patron." Joel decides

to be an artist so that he will finally be paid, and kidnaps
Kali to be his model and muse. Lewis and Vera leave together, as do the Count and Dominick.

The Bed Was Full obviously borrows from the tradition of farce, defined in The Concise Oxford Companion to
the Theatre as:

> an extreme form of comedy in which laughter
> is raised at the expense of probability.... In
> modern usage the word farce is applied to a full-
> length play dealing with some absurd situation,
> generally based on extra-marital adventures--
> hence the term, "bedroom farce."[9]

Usually, however, modern farce maintains some semblance
of realism. The characters dress and behave in a conventional manner but in the context of an absurd situation. It is from the contrast between normal response and
absurd problem that much of the humor arises. The Bed
Was Full is really a parody of farce, in which the characters often act without rational motive, playing out puns, as
when Dominick and Kali "swing" down from the loft, or following impulse, as when Kali tells Vera: "I oughta cream
you!" "Why?" asks Vera. "Because I've always wanted
to," (p. 225) is the response, especially surprising since
the characters first met moments before.

The costumes are not all described, but Kali should
be naked, and the Count, in his shirtfront but no shirt, is
also costumed in non-realistic style. The total effect is
of a bedroom farce pushed over the edge of probability into
absurdity.

Associational Clusters

According to Burke, certain points in a work, such
as beginnings and endings, may be "watershed" moments in
the work which alter or foreshadow the motivation of the
whole. The opening scene of The Bed Was Full suggests
one of the important associational clusters that will develop
through the play. The scene shows Dominick and Kali in
his studio:

> DOMINICK: Change! (KALI lies down. She
>   crosses her legs. She crosses her

> arms over her chest.)   Please!
> Something more lively.   (KALI gets
> down on all fours, swaybacked, with
> her head bowed down.)   No.   No.
> Like this! (He jumps up beside her,
> and while she keeps her preceding
> pose, he assumes a knock-kneed,
> breast-clutching, head-thrown-back,
> attitude.)   I am violated!

KALI: I am violated! (She sways back and
>   forth in her original pose.)

DOMINICK: I am violet.

KALI: I am violet.

DOMINICK: I am violent!

KALI: I am violent!

DOMINICK: I am vile!

KALI: I am vile!   (DOMINICK returns to
>   the easel.   KALI imitates his pose.)
>   (p. 210)

In this brief, comic exchange, an important associational cluster makes its first appearance.   Kali is asked to
take on, or model, several roles in order to please Dominick, the dominant male.   (The similarity between the words,
"Dominick" and "dominant" may be one of Drexler's frequent puns.)   Dominick is Kali's employer, and therefore
has economic power over her.   The pose she strikes and
keeps until the end of this exchange is "on all fours, swaybacked," suggestive of an animal.

Because Kali is swaybacked, a beast of burden is
suggested, a domestic, subservient creature.   The image of
an animal also suggests sexuality, an association that will
be made later in the play by the Count.   When Kali describes
his gloves as fawn-colored, the Count is offended because
his mother picked them out, and "a fawn is an animal and
all that implies." (p. 217).   He is offended because animals,
as natural creatures, suggest sexuality, a suggestion that he
does not want associated with mothers, who are supposed to
be completely asexual according to the stereotype.

According to this kind of stereotyping, women are
divided into the sexual type, which is degraded, and the
asexual type, which is pure.   When Kali strikes an animalistic pose, she is associated with the entirely sexual, degraded type.   An animal is also less than human, an "other"
which human beings can exploit without guilt.   Thus, this

initial image of Kali in the pose of an animal suggests subservience, a limiting sexual role, and reduction to a status
less than human, all factors contributing to women's oppression.

Dominick then gives Kali several orders: to appear
violated, violet, violent, and vile. The word "violated"
suggests woman as victim, and specifically as a victim of
rape, a role characteristic of women's oppression. The
word "violet" suggests the stereotypically frail, delicate,
idealized woman, since violet is a pale, delicate color. Violet is also a flower, suggesting an identification of woman
with passive but receptive nature. The last two images, of
woman as "violent" and "vile," cast her as the root of all
evil, a projection of male sins onto the female.

It is typical of the entire play that no one image is
developed in this scene. Rather, each is quickly named and
just as quickly dropped. Similarly, no one image of Kali
is developed in the course of the play. Instead, she is cast
and re-cast in a variety of overlapping roles by all the male
characters. All of the roles have a commonality, just as
all of Dominick's phrases contain an adjective beginning with
the letter, "v." The commonality is that all are stereotypical representations of women as less than human, existing
only in relation to men. But because each role is mentioned
only briefly, both in the first scene and in the play as a
whole, the effect is scattered and pointillistic. None of the
roles is explored or developed, but their repeated mention
finally adds up to a picture of society in which a woman,
Kali, is expected to be all things to all men, and nothing in
herself.

All of the roles overlap, both in their demands and
in the male characters who demand them. Thus, in the
first scene, to be "violent" suggests a role overlapping that
of being "vile." Dominick makes all the demands in the
first scene and many of these demands overlap those that
other male characters will make in the course of the play.
But each of the roles demanded of Kali is primarily related
to one male character. Usually, the role the male character demands is an appropriate foil to his own role.

Thus, to Dominick, Kali is primarily his model, a
physical object to be paid for and used professionally or
sexually. To the Count, an aristocrat, Kali is primarily a
servant. To Lewis, the "impotent husband" as he is de-

scribed in the list of characters, Kali is a dream, an unat-
tainable, ideal woman. To Joel, the paranoid, she is destruction. When he aspires to be an artist, she becomes
his model and muse.

Dominick invariably treats Kali as a purely physical
being, an animal useful for modelling or for sexual pleasure.
After he has ordered her to take various poses as his model,
he invites her to "swing" with him. They swing down onto
the bed, where Dominick begins making love to her. Kali
at first protests this treatment, saying, "The only use you
have for me is as a model, and now that we've fallen from
your studio, you can't keep a serious face." (p. 213) But
when he tells her that he plans to have her over again because he is working on his "woman series," she permits
Dominick to go on "painting her," now using the brush on
her body as if she were an inanimate canvas. Near the end
of the play, when Kali reveals that she has been the Count's
lover, Dominick shouts at her, "Whore, hustler, hooker,
wasn't I paying you enough?" (p. 239) Throughout the play,
Dominick's primary image of Kali is on the sensory level,
as a purely physical being.

A related image of woman as victim is developed by
the Count, who treats Kali as a servant. When he first
meets her, he orders her to pick up his gloves off the floor.
Later, when she begins tidying the room, he says to Kali,
"I thought I told you to have my shirts ready." "You told
who?" she responds. He says, "Oh, forgive me, for a moment I was lost in time. You remind me of the laundress
who claimed to be my real mother." (p. 217) To the Count,
Kali is a servant, woman as the inferior and victim of man.

The Count also associates Kali as laundress with his
mother in this statement, creating a comment on the mother-
ing role. As the moral and social educators of the young,
mothers are supposed to have a moral superiority and an
elevated position in the society. The Count's defense of his
mother against animalistic associations, mentioned earlier,
bears out this image. But as housekeepers, mothers are
also the society's servants, performing tasks that are considered menial by comparison with men's wage-earning work.
The Count's image of Kali is as a member of an inferior
societal caste, that of the servant-mother, an association
that appears on both the familial and the abstract level.

Lewis is the only man who asks Kali who she is,

rather than telling her. But she responds by striking a series of suggestive poses, which seems to establish her in
his mind as a sort of a dream girl, like the pin-ups in magazines. This image develops the same association as Dominick's statement that Kali is "violet," ethereal. Lewis
threatens to kiss Kali's nose, but later admits that this is
also a dream: he can't really kiss noses; he just pretends.
When Joel prepares to kidnap her, Lewis stakes a counter-
claim on Kali, saying, "In my dreams she belongs to me."
(p. 241) To Lewis, too, Kali appears on the abstract level,
as the girl of his dreams.

Joel primarily regards Kali, as her name suggests,
as the Indian goddess of destruction. "Take me if you must,
but don't torture me! Oh great goddess, I am not worthy of
your hundred-prong pointed deaths," (p. 216) he says to
her. His image of her is the "vile" and "violent" one suggested by Dominick in the first scene. It is also one of
magical power. At the end of the play, when Joel proposes
that Kali model for him, he tells her: "I've been spying on
you, and whosoever you team up with becomes a great man.
Please come away with me and bless my studio." (p. 240)

Note that the image of Kali as beneficent muse over-
laps that of Lewis's ideal dream girl. Similarly, the Count
is not the only character to regard Kali as nursemaid and
mother. Dominick comes to her to get a splinter removed
from his hand, and Joel to get his cut bandaged. All of the
roles are demanded of her by more than one character, and
none is elaborated at length. Instead, each association is
like one dot in a pointillistic painting. The total picture
created is the objectification of Kali.

Most of the associations in this cluster are either on
the sensory level or the abstract level, since all the men in
the play perceive Kali's role either as purely physical or as
purely symbolic. Nearly all the description of Kali in the
play is uttered by these men; she seldom describes herself,
nor does her behavior suggest a fixed character.

Each of the other characters, male and female, has
a one-dimensional, farcical role which he or she maintains
throughout the drama. Vera is the wife suspected of infidel-
ity; the Count is her dashing, aristocratic lover. Joel is
the paranoid detective hired by Lewis, the impotent husband,
to spy on the unfaithful wife. Dominick is the narcissistic,
arrogant artist in his studio "above" the bourgeois bedroom

farce in which the rest engage. Kali does, of course, have
a role, but significantly, it is that of the artist's model.
As the play progresses, she is asked to "model" various
roles for the male characters, but she never adopts a fixed
character.

The male characters, in contrast to Kali, establish
an associative cluster around themselves through their own
words and actions, rather than primarily through what others
say about them. While each of the men in the play has his
own identifiable characteristics, such as Dominick's narcis-
sism, the Count's vanity, or Joel's paranoia, they also share
a cluster of associations. This cluster includes associations
with violence, with helplessness, and with self-hatred.

The violence in the cluster surrounding male characters is both physical and verbal. Verbally, male characters
make threats, such as Joel's: "Vera, do you hear? Evil
betrayer of singular behavior. Do you hear your accuser
and tremble? Enter into the Kingdom of Jezamehatmacong
and repent!" (p. 216) When Kali suggests that she and
Dominick get married, Dominick responds that she will have
to cut herself first, and the Count offers the stiletto in his
cane for this purpose. Physically, fights among the male
characters are frequent: Joel and the Count fight over the
Count's glove; the Count and Lewis fight when Joel produces
evidence that the Count has cuckolded Lewis; Joel fights with
himself in the mirror.

The helplessness included in the cluster of associations surrounding men in the play is reflected in their frequent pleas for help. Joel cuts his hand and pleads for help
in stopping the bleeding. Dominick gets a splinter and pleads
for help in removing it. Lewis, when asked for assistance,
starts walking on and off the bed, explaining that he is suffering and doesn't know what to do. In each of these cases,
Kali relieves the suffering character, playing a "nurse" or
"mother" role. She gives Joel a glove to use as a bandage;
she removes Dominick's splinter, and she offers to kiss
Lewis on the nose, distracting him from his pacing.

The self-hatred in this cluster develops from Joel's
fight with himself in the mirror and his attitude that he is
"not worthy" of death at Kali's hands, to the Count's comment when Kali says they are all doomed: "We are, but
who cares?" (p. 238) Joel contributes further to this cluster by competing with himself at broadjumping, and losing.

Elements of this cluster appear on all three of the
levels described by Burke: the sensory, the familial, and
the abstract. On the sensory level are the examples of
physical violence between competing males or, as in Joel's
case, directed against himself. On the personal, familial
level is the male characters' casting of Kali in the role of
mother and nurse by protesting their helplessness to her.
The Count's "who cares" attitude, because it expresses a
general philosophy, is on the abstract level. The men's
threats of violence are also on the abstract level, because
they are symbolic bids for power rather than physical acts.

The two primary associational clusters in the play,
then, form around the male characters, showing them to be
violent, self-hating, and helpless, and around the male characters' images of Kali, which they attempt to force on her.
Vera, the only other female character, plays a stable role
largely identified with the male characters. Her character
description is "the wife of Lewis." (p. 209) Because she
acts within this stereotypical role, she is largely a passive
character, explaining to Lewis that "men decide. Women
abide." (p. 218) She does engage in one conflict, a fight
with Kali over the Count. This action suits her role as unfaithful wife and strengthens her identification with men.

The socio-sexual hierarchy of the play is one in which
men have power, maintained by threats of violence, which
they use to force women into roles in relation to them, as
their nurses, wives, lovers, goddesses, servants, mothers,
or models. In each instance, these roles are objectifications
of women, in which they are not autonomous subjects but
tools existing for men's purposes. Vera accepts this hierarchy, playing her role of passive but unfaithful wife. Kali
is the only character who does not fit into a specific role
in the hierarchy of the play. Instead of accepting a role as
Vera does, she constantly evades the men's attempts to cast
her. Her repeated, decreasingly effective attempts at evasion make up the pattern of symbolic action of the play.

Pattern of Symbolic Action

The opening exchange of The Bed Was Full suggests
not only associational clusters in the play, but also its pattern of symbolic action. In the opening scene, Kali at first
resists Dominick's orders by repeating them without changing
her pose. On his last command, she finally adopts the pose

he has demanded of her. In the same way, the pattern of
symbolic action reveals repeated demands from the male
characters that Kali adopt stereotypical roles, demands Kali
attempts to resist but is finally forced to meet when she is
kidnapped by Joel.

       Kali's response to the demands of the male charac-
ters falls into a pattern. In the first part of the play, Kali
defies them, corrects the men trying to cast her into roles,
and acts autonomously, according to her own inclination. In
the middle section of the play, she attempts to ally herself
with various male characters, but evades them again when
they try to control her behavior. At the end of the play,
she defies Joel's attempt to make her his model, but is defeated when he kidnaps her at gunpoint.

       In the first section of the play, Kali acts freely, unin-
timidated by attempts to cast her in a role. When Dominick orders her into a variety of poses as his model, she
eventually gets bored and stops modelling for him. When
the Count orders her to pick up his gloves, she says that
she will not, "because I threw them down." (p. 215) When
she is threatened by Joel, she reminds him that she is Kali:
"I destroy." (p. 216) But when Joel immediately casts her
as the goddess of destruction, she evades this role, too, explaining that "I wouldn't dream of destroying an old school-
mate." (p. 216) When the Count reminds her to have his
shirts ready, she denies being his laundress. And when
Lewis asks her who she is, she strikes a series of poses,
suggesting that she is a model, but also suggesting that she
does not wish to be limited to a single role.

       In the next several scenes, Kali attempts to relate
to the men in the play, but evades them again when they
respond by casting her into stereotypical roles. First she
offers Joel the Count's glove as a bandage for his cut hand.
Joel responds: "Not all women are bad." (p. 224) Kali
withdraws from him at once, evading his attempt to cast her
as the rare good woman, the helpful nurse. Kali then tries
to ally herself with the Count, saying that she is in love
with him, but when the Count says, "You can have me,"
(p. 227) she loses interest in this role as well. She offers
to marry Dominick next, but when he tells her she must cut
herself first, casting her in the role of suffering wife, Kali
abandons the idea of marriage.

       In the final section of the play, Kali is finally forced

to adopt a role permanently, that of Joel's model and muse.
She resists this role strenuously, telling Joel to "shut up
and go away." (p. 240) She wavers momentarily when he
urges her to "Fulfill your destiny, butterfly," (p. 241) but
finally refuses him absolutely. The other male characters
then try vainly to claim her once more:

>   COUNT: She's mine.
>   DOMINICK: There was a time ...
>   LEWIS: In my dreams she belongs to me (p.
>   241)

But Joel adds the final element to the associations of violence surrounding men in the play by drawing a gun and
dragging Kali offstage. The pattern of symbolic action shows
Kali defeated by the demands of the play's socio-sexual hierarchy represented by Joel, despite her evasive resistance.

Agent:Scene Ratio

Because threatened violence gives power to the oppressive male class in the socio-sexual hierarchy, and because Kali wavers in her resistance to this class, scene
dominates the play. Kali, the agent, resists only by evading,
never by open defiance, and sometimes attempts momentarily
to ally herself with the hierarchy. Her weakness of motivation, gradually revealed in the pattern of symbolic action,
is summed up at a critical point in the scene in which Joel
begs Kali to come to his studio. At first she resists, but
she does waver before finally refusing him again. He then
resorts to violence, drawing his gun and kidnapping her.
Her moment of weakness combined with his threat of violence at this critical point demonstrate the reasons for Kali's
defeat.

When scene dominates the ratio, Burke says that the
play should be allied to the philosophic school of materialism. In the materialistic philosophy, spirit is reduced to
matter, and the individual is subject to a deterministic environment. In The Bed Was Full, despite its farcical style,
the conclusion is deterministic.

In the course of the play, it becomes obvious that
Kali cannot fulfill the multitude of roles demanded of her.
Her oppressors do not fully develop any one of these de-
mands. But the continuous addition of more and more de-

manded roles, like dots in a painting eventually overlapping
one another, finally creates the picture of a socio-sexual
hierarchy impossible to transcend.   The multitude of roles
demanded of a single character make it impossible for Kali
to achieve autonomy.   Kali, the agent, is reduced from an
individual to the actor of stereotypical roles, from spirit to
physical object, by the socio-sexual hierarchy of the play.

Thus, as is common in farce, the status quo is re-
stored at the end of the play.   But it is an imperfect status
quo, an unjust order which Kali has attempted unsuccess-
fully to resist.   Her kidnapping is an involuntary sacrifice
to the unjust hierarchy, the inevitable fate of an individual
who has not willingly conformed to any of the roles offered
to her, but who has not succeeded in transcending or over-
throwing the prevailing order.   The ruling male class, represented by Joel, will necessarily exercise its power to
force her into a materialistic role as physical object.

Conclusion

Although The Bed Was Full seems at first reading to
be as nonsensical as it is funny, it does have a coherent
pattern of symbolic action.   This pattern is made up of the
agent's attempts to resist the unjust socio-sexual hierarchy
established by the play's clusters of associations.   Kali's
weakness combined with the violence controlled by the ruling
male class in the hierarchy determine her eventual defeat.
Because the scene, the socio-sexual hierarchy, dominates,
the play is allied to the materialistic philosophy.

Richard Gilman, in the introduction to Drexler's
plays, says:

> Drexler's imagination holds that the world is for-
> ever trying to impose roles and identities upon us
> which it is our duty to resist and repudiate, by
> outwitting the identifiers and the casting direc-
> tors....   Continually causing one another to lose
> footing, slipping on each other's banana peels,
> turning up in each other's beds, clothes, baths,
> and mirrors, [her characters] make up new worlds
> of farce whose highly serious intention, as in all
> true examples of the genre, is to liberate us from
> the way things are said to be. [10]

In The Bed Was Full, the play's "highly serious intention"
is to satirize the socio-sexual hierarchy, represented by a
multitude of stereotyped roles, and to show woman's futile
attempt to establish her autonomy within such an unjust hierarchy.

Notes

1. Joan Goulianos, "Women and the Avant-Garde Theatre,"
   in Woman: An Issue, eds. Lee R. Edwards, Mary
   Heath and Lisa Baskin (Boston: Little, Brown & Co.,
   1972), p. 266.

2. Ibid.

3. Sara Sanborn, review of The Cosmopolitan Girl, New
   York Times, 30 March 1975, sec. 7, p. 5.

4. New York Times, 20 May 1973, sec. 2, p. 1.

5. Arthur Sainer, "Rosalyn Drexler," in Contemporary
   Dramatists, ed. James Vinson (New York: St. James
   Press, 1973), p. 209.

6. Rosalyn Drexler, "The New Androgyny," Vogue, February 1977, p. 94.

7. Sainer, p. 208.

8. Rosalyn Drexler, "The Bed Was Full," in The Line of
   Least Existence and Other Plays (New York: Random
   House, 1967), p. 210. Subsequent page references
   to The Bed Was Full in this chapter will be in parentheses following the quotation in the text.

9. Phyllis Hartnoll, ed., The Concise Oxford Companion
   to the Theatre (London: Oxford University Press,
   1972), p. 170.

10. Richard Gilman, introduction to The Line of Least
    Existence and Other Plays, p. xi.

CHAPTER 3

IN THE BOOM BOOM ROOM

Introduction

David Rabe's In the Boom Boom Room* is the story
of Chrissy, a Philadelphia go-go dancer struggling to be
recognized as fully human by her society. The associational
clusters in the play reveal a highly structured, completely
inflexible patriarchy. Within this patriarchy, all the characters must interrelate according to limited sexual roles.
Chrissy's symbolic actions are increasingly intense attempts
to be recognized and to interact with others outside of these
roles. Her rising anger eventually meets with violent reprisal, however, and the play ends with Chrissy submitting
to the patriarchy, having adopted a new and more humiliat-
ing role as a topless dancer.

The philosophic conclusions of the play are strongly
deterministic. Rabe seems to have written the play, not as
a political statement, but as a personal attempt to empathize
with the plight of woman as object. In a 1973 interview, he
said of the play, "... whatever I accomplished, I know that
the basic thing I was trying to do was very personal and in
terms of solving a distance between myself and women, and
trying to go through all that. And I did. I mean, I feel an
enormous difference now."[1] The play succeeds on these
terms, but does not suggest that there is any solution, even
a personal one, to the societal problem it depicts.

Biography

David Rabe was born on March 10, 1940, in Dubuque,
Iowa. He attended Laras College, a Catholic institution in
Dubuque, where he began writing short stories and plays.
After graduation, he began a master's degree in theatre at

---

*In the Boom Boom Room by David Rabe (New York: Al-
fred A. Knopf, 1975). Quotes from this play reprinted by
permission.

Villanova University in Pennsylvania, but dropped out after
two years and supported himself with odd jobs while trying
to establish himself as a writer. In 1965, he was drafted.

          For the last eleven months of his two-year military
service, Rabe was assigned to a hospital unit at Long Binh,
South Vietnam, where he served as a guard, clerk, driver,
and construction worker. On his return to the U. S., Rabe
resumed his studies at Villanova, where a professor arranged
for him to receive the balance of an uncompleted Rockefeller
grant. Rabe recalls that when he returned from Vietnam, he
wanted to write a novel about his experiences.

> But then I chanced upon a grant of money, a
> Rockefeller grant in playwrighting, enough to
> live on for a year and a half. I remember
> thinking, "I'll dash off some plays real quick,
> then focus in on the novel."
> But when I sat down to write, regardless of
> the form, I found it impossible to avoid the things
> most crowding my mind, and because these mem-
> ories and ideas were of such extreme value to
> me, I could deal with them with nothing less than
> my best effort.
> What I am trying to say is simply that if things
> had turned out differently, I don't know if I would
> have written what I have in the way I have, but
> the grant was a playwrighting grant. [2]

Since then, Rabe has supported himself by writing and sometimes by teaching playwrighting at the university level.

          He is usually associated with plays showing the hor-
rors of war, but Rabe objects to applying the term "anti-
war play" to his work.

> Finally, in my estimation, an "antiwar" play
> is one that expects, by the very fabric of its
> executed conception, to have political effect. I
> anticipated no such consequences from my plays,
> nor did I conceive them in the hope that they
> would have such consequences. [3]

He goes on to say that a play's large-scale political effect
is doubtful and that he hopes his plays have more content
than do political tracts. Finally, he points out that plays
showing a family, a marriage, young people, or crime un-

favorably are not called "antifamily," "antimarriage," "anti-
youth," or "anticrime" plays. "I think these labels do not
exist because family, marriage, youth, and crime are all
viewed as phenomena permanently a part of the eternal human pageant. I believe war to be an equally permanent part
of that pageant."[4] No doubt, Rabe would respond similarly
to attempts to read politically feminist views into Boom
Boom Room.

Rabe's other plays are The Basic Training of Pavlo
Hummel, written in 1968, which received an Obie Award;
Sticks and Bones, also 1968, which received a Tony; The
Orphan, 1973; and Streamers, 1976, which received a New
York Drama Critics Award. In the Boom Boom Room first
opened at Lincoln Center's Vivian Beaumont Theater in 1973,
and was produced by Joseph Papp as all Rabe's plays have
been. The play was plagued with production problems, and
opened to mixed reviews. Stanley Kauffmann's review in
The New Republic was particularly negative:

> The theme, the ravaging of a female social-sexual
> victim, is so familiar that one counts on the fa-
> miliarity, in a way: one assumes that the author
> would never have chosen it unless he was convinced
> he had new insights or an artistic vision of the
> subject that in itself would provide new insights....
> Not so. Not Rabe. Clearly, one can say after
> the fourth experience of him, his notion of play-
> writing is to get a clever device, impressively
> flashy, than just fill in the rest of the play as
> needed. [5]

Several reviews, however, praised Madeline Kahn in the
leading role. Kahn herself gave some of the credit for her
portrayal to Rabe. In an interview with him in the New York
Times, she said:

> The most amazing thing to me when reading it and
> doing it--you know, knowing it was written by a
> man, by you--was that you gave me, the woman,
> every opportunity to display so many sides of my-
> self, including rage, anger, real all-out rage. [6]

It is interesting to note, in evaluating the play, that
critics have objected as Kauffmann did to the triviality and
familiarity of the theme and character. When the play,
somewhat rewritten, reopened in New York at the Anspacher
Theater in 1974, the New York Times reviewer commented:

> What the playwright has done--especially in this
> new and better focused version of the script--is to
> offer the portrait of a woman. The central fault
> of the play is that the woman herself, one of na-
> ture's losers, is just not very interesting.[7]

Such objections were not widely raised in response to Rabe's
war plays, although they also frequently depict "nature's
losers." Rabe has said, "The specificity of my work certainly comes out of my experience. You're obsessed with
certain things and you write about them. But I don't think
my real obsession is the Vietnam War. The world of 'Boom
Boom Room' illuminates the real nature of the other plays."[8]
In other words, he seems to suggest that his underlying
theme of the horrifying hopelessness of existence is better
expressed in Boom Boom Room than in his more overtly violent war plays. Furthermore, Rabe sees a similarity between the Army environment and the world of go-go bars.
"There was the same sense of proximate violence and the
same sense of indiscriminate behavior being acceptable," he
told the New York Times.[9]

Rabe's most recent play, Streamers, has also been
among his most successful. Asked to comment on strongly
negative audience reactions to the violence in Streamers,
Rabe responded, "It's like I must be doing something right,
finally [in getting such negative reactions]; to make violence
unbearable, not salable."[10]

Walter Kerr, in evaluating Rabe's work to date, said
that there is in all his plays an element of despair:

> Mr. Rabe has a consistent view of his troubled
> universe, and whether that view is right or wrong,
> there is something intuitively unpalatable to a good
> many spectators somewhere inside it.... The ac-
> tual message, if I read it correctly, is this. We
> are all--black, white, straight, queer, parents,
> children, friends, foes, stable, unstable--living
> together in the same "house." And we can't do
> it.... And so, to the degree that we admire the
> play, to the degree that we believe in it, we de-
> spair.[11]

Like Rabe's other plays, Boom Boom Room is an essentially
despairing work, full of compassion over the impossibility of
our living together.

Plot Summary

In the Boom Boom Room concerns a go-go dancer,
Chrissy, who works in Big Tom's Boom Boom Room.   She
has moved to a new apartment since getting this job, and
acquires new acquaintances, including Guy, a gay man who
lives upstairs; Al and Ralphie, who follow her home from
the Boom Boom Room; Eric, who has seen her dance and
wants to date her; and Susan, the announcer at the go-go
bar.   Chrissy's parents also find out her new address and
come to visit her there.

As the series of scenes in the go-go bar, Chrissy's
apartment, and her parents' home progresses, Chrissy becomes angry and frustrated.   None of the people she meets
seems to regard her as a person.   Susan offers her friendship, but also propositions her sexually.   Chrissy and Guy
begin a friendship based on their mutual sense of exploitation
by men, but the accompanying sense of competition quickly
drives them apart.   Finally, Chrissy decides to marry Al
because:

> I don't know how it happens, but a woman is ten-
> derness and love.   Just tenderness and love no
> matter what her body.   I don't even know if what
> I'm talkin' about sometimes ever even really hap-
> pened, but I am gonna be dedicated to the one I
> love.   We'll be married and regular and I'll be
> happy having' a life fixin' the terrible hurt in Al
> so he's happy. [12]

In the next scene, Chrissy and Al are quarreling.
The argument escalates into sexual taunts and finally Chrissy
mentions "niggers."   When she sees Al's response, she begins threatening to have sex with blacks, enraging Al, who
beats Chrissy as the scene ends.   At the end of the play,
Chrissy, wearing a mask, is dancing topless, something she
swore earlier in the play never to do.

Associational Clusters

The associations in Boom Boom Room form several
clusters: around food, around dancing and other sexual display, around violence, and around the paternal (and patriarchal) relation.   Elements of these clusters appear on all

three levels of meaning: the sensory, the familial, and the
abstract.   The initial references to elements of all of the
play's clusters of associations are in the first scene.

        The first two characters introduced in Boom Boom
Room are Chrissy and her father, Harold.   The play begins
when her father breaks into her apartment, interrupting
Chrissy's dance practice and frightening her.   Even when
she recognizes her father, her uneasy manner does not
change.

        Harold accuses Chrissy of having gotten the apart-
ment so that she can entertain men: "Blond boys, dark-
haired ones, Spanish spics--hot bloods, black boys--big
cocks. I know. Rumours." (pp. 2-3) She offers him a
sandwich.   He describes his recent hospital stay.   He hated
the hospital and his roommate there, but liked his roommate's flowers, which he destroyed by poking at them while
his roommate slept.   He recalls having chased Chrissy with
a belt when she was a little girl, but Chrissy says it was
her uncles who chased her.   Finally Harold leaves, telling
Chrissy she has a lot of spirit.

        In this first, brief scene, the play's important asso-
ciations are introduced on all three levels of meaning.   On
the sensory level, Chrissy is associated with providing food,
Harold with eating.   Chrissy is dancing as the play opens,
observed by her father.   Harold and his brothers are described as inflicting violence, Chrissy as suffering it.

        On the familial level, Harold's reference to the race
of Chrissy's supposed boyfriends is an association between
race and sex that will recur in the climactic scene of violence at the end of the play.   The association is on the familial level because race is a kind of extended family.   References to race as the play continues invariably link it to
sex.   Because a black man and a white woman, both members of low castes, can form a relationship in which the
white man is extraneous, miscegenation is seen as a defiance
of the white patriarchy.   But the most significant familial
relationship is between Chrissy and Harold, daughter and
father.   Burke has pointed out that the placement of associations is as important as their number.   By placing a father-
daughter relationship in the opening scene and by introducing
that relationship as if it were one of a prowler and his victim, Rabe gives meaning to the paternal relationship throughout the play.

On the abstract level, this relationship is a patriarchal one. Harold, representative of men in the play, has
power enforced by his capacity for violence which permeates
all the relationships between men and women in the play.
The hospital stay described in the first scene is only the
initial instance of men in association with hospitals, prisons,
the army, and the church--all institutions about which Chrissy
is curious, but which she never enters. Even the experience of being a prisoner or a patient gives men in the play
a certain power. Ralphie boasts of his prowess at surviving
jail sentences: "Day a the week comes I can't do ninety
days in jail standin' on my head, I look for different work. "
(p. 20) Later, Al boasts that he has overheard secrets
from the doctors while hospitalized for "drinking disease":
"Many things to be learned in a hospital for he of the alert
ear and eye, such as me. " (p. 93) Thus, on the abstract
level, men are inside the institutions of power in the play;
women are outside.

The associations established in the first scene recur
and develop as the play continues, but do not change. On
the sensory level, Harold continues to associate his daughter
with food for his consumption. He shows Chrissy a tomato
plant he is planning to grow and later eat. "Givin' somethin' life gives you that right, don't you think?" (p. 72), he
asks her. Chrissy, who used to work at the A & P, continues to associate herself with food by offering to feed her
father and later Al, and by carrying a thermos of coffee
around to offer people in hopes that this will make them like
her better. Chrissy's mother is similarly associated with
offering food. She tells Chrissy that the way to a man's
heart is through his stomach. Her mother is seen buying
groceries, fixing Kool-Aid, and making chocolate pudding for
her husband. Thus, the association with food expands from
just Chrissy and her father to an association of women as
food for men's consumption.

Chrissy's go-go dancing, which opens the play, is
another sensory image that develops further into images of
women displayed and adorned for the benefit of men. In the
first scene, Harold spies on Chrissy while she is dancing.
In later scenes, Al, Ralphie, and Eric are all attracted to
her because of her dancing. Susan gives her dancing lessons
in which she explains that doing the "Jerk" should look like
getting punched in the stomach and straightening up again.
That, according to Susan, is what men like to see: women
displaying themselves, "arrogant," and then knocked down,

humiliated. The other go-go dancers give Chrissy advice on
displaying herself to men:

> SALLY: And somethin' else, don't be learnin'
> only the down and dirty dances.
> MELISSA: Sometimes it's coyness they want--or
> they want us dancing coquettishly.
> VIKKI: Frivolous.
> SALLY: Christ, I need another shower already.
> VIKKI: I smell like a skunk; an' I'm all outa
> Jean Nate.
> MELISSA: You know Chrissy, if you're dancin'
> and chewin' gum like I saw you, you
> gotta keep it under your tongue. I
> mean, it keeps your breath nice, but it
> looks disgusting. (pp. 17-18)

At one point, Chrissy herself despairs of ever achieving
the multitude of sensory details that will make her attractive.

> I gotta be makin' some resolutions about my stu-
> pid life. I can't not bite my fingernails. I can't
> not do it. I can't keep 'em long and red, because
> I'm a person and I'm a nervous person, and I diet
> and diet I might as well eat a barrel a marshmal-
> lows. My voice is not sexy or appealing. I try
> to raise it. I try to lower it. I got a list of
> good things to say to a man in bed. I say stupid
> stuff made up outa my head. My hands are too
> big. My stockings bag all the time. Nothin' keeps
> me a man I want anyway. I mean, how'm I gonna
> look like that? (Seizing a glamour magazine, she
> thrusts the cover, the face of a beautiful woman,
> at him.) I can't do it. Not ever. (p. 47)

Later, however, she temporarily regains hope, believing
that if she wears her hair differently or perhaps buys new
underwear, she can be attractive to men.

On all three levels of meaning, violent words and
acts recur throughout the play, gradually increasing in seriousness. From the first scene in which Harold nostagically
recalls chasing Chrissy with a belt, the described acts of
violence escalate. On the sensory level, Susan describes
seeing a man cut another one open with a razor blade. Al
describes leaving his second wife when he began wanting to
kill the household pets. Ralphie, Al's lunatic sidekick, re-

marks in a characteristic non sequitur, "Life is all like
World War II." (p. 26) Susan tells about having revenged
herself when jilted by her high-school boyfriend. Her re-
venge was to shoot him. Finally, the violence in the play
emerges onstage when Al beats Chrissy just before the end
of the play.

On the familial level, the relationship between Harold
and Chrissy is the first one introduced, and the most significant. The violent, patriarchal relationship, which is significant on the abstract level as well, imbues all the male-fe-
male relationships in the play. Chrissy, the daughter who
shares her associations with feeding men and displaying one-
self for men with the other women in the play, also shares
with them her associations with serving as men's victim.
The go-go girls describe boyfriends who "hurt them a hundred times a day." Chrissy's mother says that her father
"had women sittin' down with coat hangers all across this
state," (p. 75) aborting themselves after affairs with him
because he did not like birth control. On the abstract level,
the go-go dancers discuss their ideal, a go-go dancer named
Jennifer whom Big Eddie used to pay two hundred dollars to
dance to "Lovin' Feelin'." Chrissy dreams of achieving this
ideal: "Gonna be so much helpless dancin' tenderness they're
just gonna all wanna wrap me up in all their money." (p. 19)
This image combines women displaying themselves, men with
the power to "buy" women like commodities, and the victimization of women who must be "helpless" in order to be a
valued commodity.

All the men in the play share the power associated
with Harold, the violent patriarch. Eric is concerned that
he will not be able to dominate Chrissy until he has had
sex with her. Ralphie makes the connection between himself
and Harold by telling Chrissy that he is in mental contact
with her father (whom he does not, in fact, know) and that
her father tells him what to say to her. Chrissy herself
finally makes the connection between her father and all men
explicit. She calls her husband, Al, "Daddyo," and addresses him as if he were her father, accusing him of having
put her "in a woman he didn't love," (p. 108) that is, of
having impregnated her mother. She has made the connection between father and husband, and among all men as patriarchal oppressors.

The abstract representation of man as patriarch is
developed in religious imagery by Eric and Ralphie. Ralphie,

46   Feminist Drama

while threatening Chrissy with his supposed connection to
her father, refers also to God the father, who knows everything that Chrissy does. He tries to force her to eat ketch-
up, telling her that it is his blood, a kind of communion
which he can administer as a patriarchal representative of
her father, her father in heaven, and men in general. Eric
struggles with religion on a more sophisticated level, arguing
at first that "Mother Church" has always oppressed him because he is a man. He believes that Mother Church is a
force for castration since priests can attain authority in the
church only by being celibate. Eric can oppose castration,
he finally decides, by having sex with Chrissy and then con-
fessing the act:

> And then, in the morning just before mass, in
> the confessional, I'll kneel beside old Father Kerr,
> only the wicker confessional wall between us. And
> I'll whisper of your power.... And he will tell
> the prayers of penance that will cleanse me of all
> dark cruel longing, the mystery of you. All mys-
> tery of you. (p. 36)

In other words, the power of the church is Father Kerr's,
an essentially patriarchal power like all the power in the
play. Eric can, by asserting his masculinity with Chrissy,
be cleansed of the power of feminine sexuality through con-
fession in the church.[13]

      Other institutions, like the church, are male pre-
serves in the play. Chrissy asks Al and Ralphie to tell
about their prison stay. She is curious since her father
and uncles have all been there and she has not. Chrissy
considers seeking help from the medical institution in psychiatric counseling. But she tells Susan she could never go
to a woman counselor, although Susan warns her about male
counselors, saying that the word is a pun: "therapist" equal-
ling "the rapist." All institutions are controlled by men,
closed to women or a threat to them.

      Thus, the clusters of associations in the play, taken
together, depict a patriarchal society, an unjust socio-sexual
hierarchy against which Chrissy finally rebels. The association of men with power and women with victimization in
the play is not complete, however. In general, men inflict
violence; women suffer its consequences or are left out entirely. For instance, Chrissy's childhood memories include
coming upon a window while playing at night:

> a TV ... was there and there was a army movie
> on it with this actor John Agar playing a wounded
> soldier.   The man in the kitchen was very fat....
> Then the man started yelling, "Get out, get out!"
> And this head of this woman who was his wife was
> appearing a little into the doorway.   "Get out,
> please, get out," he kept yelling and he never
> looked away from the TV on which these huge can-
> nons were firing.   So I ran for fear I would be
> seen ..." (p. 40)

Clearly, the violent war movie with its cannon firing is a
male association in the play, representing a world from
which women are fearfully excluded.   But two characters,
Susan and Guy, form an apparent exception to this association.

        Susan represents a reversal of the association of men
with the perpetration of violence.   In her most significant
speech, she says that her high school boyfriend had made
her take off her clothes, and then had covered her with
butter before leaving her for another girl.   The association
between women as food (covered with butter) and men as
consumers is the same sensory association that runs through
the play.   But Susan's response to this humiliation is a new
departure:

> I shot him.   I didn't know you could be shot and
> not die, so I didn't shoot him any more.   I just
> walked away.   He lived and went on to play Big
> Ten football after a year delay.   It's somethin',
> though, how once you shoot a man, they're none
> of them the same any more, and you know how
> easy, if you got a gun, they fall down. (p. 31)

Susan has learned from this experience to be the aggressor
instead of the victim.   She propositions Chrissy sexually,
stepping outside the passive female role.   When Chrissy
seeks Susan later, however, she finds her in bed with a man.
When Chrissy decides to marry, she is partly motivated by
her fear of ending up like Susan.   "I'll be for him, and
that way I'll never end up like her.   Like Susan: A man in
disguise." (p. 97)

        Unfortunately, Susan is "a man in disguise" in the
sense that she has simply reversed the oppressor-victim
role in her own case, and has become as much of an op-

pressor as the men in the play. She is no more autonomous than Chrissy in the sense of being independent of the
socio-sexual hierarchy. She is still sexually involved with
men, and more importantly, she perceives Chrissy as everyone else in the play does, strictly in sexual terms. Her
only unique quality is her ability to oppress women as a
man would do, based on her discovery of the power of violence. Once Susan has shot her boyfriend and has understood how to use violence for her own ends, she gains a
more privileged position in the hierarchy, but without per-
ceiving its injustice or rebelling against the existing order.

Guy, Chrissy's gay neighbor, is the other apparent
exception to the hierarchical rule of men as oppressors,
women as victims in the play. Guy admires the costume
Chrissy has made to dance in, "like a Playboy bunny suit,
see, except I'm makin' fur on it and softer. The real ones
[bunny suits] are very mean. I don't want no mean one."
(p. 11) Guy even makes himself a costume like Chrissy's
to wear to a gay costume ball. Thus, Guy is associated
with vulnerability and ornamentation, otherwise feminine associations in the play.

Because both Guy and Chrissy have been jilted by
men, they have a sense of kinship. Guy agrees with Chrissy
that men have no sensitivity, and suggests to her that they
each seek men for sex, "And we'll come back here to tell
one another of their stupidity--their peculiarity. All affec-
tion, all tender feeling will be reserved for us." (p. 49)
Unfortunately, Guy and Chrissy also share a need to be attractive commodities to men. Both of them dream of being
a Playboy centerfold, "posed on fur." As a result, their
friendship quickly degenerates into bitter rivalry. Guy, like
Susan, has found a place in the hierarchy with the opposite
sex. But he is still a part of the hierarchy, and because
he is, he cannot perceive Chrissy as other than a sexual
rival. Neither Susan nor Guy is capable of responding to
Chrissy as a full human being because both are still willing
participants in the socio-sexual hierarchy, although they have
found unusual positions within it.

This hierarchy is summed up in Susan's description
of the three nightclubs owned by Big Tom: the Boom Boom
Room, where women dance for men; the Room Thomasita,
where men dance for men; and the Tom-Tom Room, where
women dance for women. All three are owned by Big Tom,
who makes the rounds of his bars each night: "He wanders

all three like a man through a single home, making sure the
jukebox songs are current, the customers grinning, the hook-
ers polite and busy." (p. 58)   Like this complex of go-go
bars, the society of the play allows some variation in the
sex of those who display themselves and those who pay to
watch.   But everyone falls into one of the two categories;
no one has more than a stereotypical, sexual role, "mounter" or "mounted" in the hierarchy.   And the real power is
in the hands of the man symbolized here by Big Tom, the
patriarchal figure dominating the entire system.   This system, revealed in the clusters of associations in the play,
does not change.

Pattern of Symbolic Action

        The pattern of symbolic action in the play does
change and evolve, however.   Boom Boom Room falls into
a pattern of Chrissy encountering each of the other characters, one by one.   Each character attempts to impose a
limiting, sexual role on Chrissy, forcing her to accept her
place in the status quo, a process she resists more and
more violently as the play progresses.   She seems to give
in suddenly to their attempts when she decides to marry,
but she immediately returns to her highest pitch of rebellion in the next scene, followed by her being beaten and a
return to the status quo.

        In the first act, Chrissy does not yet realize that
the environment makes it impossible for her to be recognized as a full human being.   Harold tells her in the first
scene, "I'm a permanent fixture." (p. 4)   This statement
is true of him as representative of the entire, unjust hierarchy.   But Chrissy responds optimistically: "I'll just keep
after some things I can maybe get is sort of all I'm saying." (p. 3)   She is as yet unaware of the deterministic nature of her surroundings.   In the next scenes, as Chrissy
meets Guy, Eric, and Al, she feels some irritation only at
Eric, and her irritation is specific and personal.   When he
apologizes for not having paid attention to her by saying that
he is in mental therapy, she responds:

                Well, Eric, that's too bad and everything but
                when you are trying to be with a person who
                has dances in her head all the time, and who
                is a special kind of person--I mean, I have
                dreamed of ballet all my life and other kinds

> of dancing-so-you-tell-a-story! Of which go-go
> is just a poor facsimile--and that kind of person
> must be treated very specially, or they will get
> upset with you as I just did, and maybe even yell
> at you. (p. 16)

Chrissy is asserting her autonomy here, but she is describing the situation in purely personal terms, based on her
special needs.

     With Al, Chrissy asserts herself only to the extent
to insisting on birth control because "I was nearly a abortion
in my mother, so I don't wanna ever have one on anybody
else!" (p. 27) With Susan, she admits a fear of men, but
does not respond to the anger behind Susan's story of shoot-
ing her boyfriend. And in her second scene with Eric, she
protests only mildly: "I got stuff to say, too, Eric. I'm
sayin' some stuff, too, ain't I?" (p. 34) The act ends with
Chrissy responding lovingly to Al's definition of her in purely
sexual terms. "You're the best lay I ever had in a long
time," he tells her. And she answers, "Oh, Al, I love
you," (p. 37) still essentially acceptant of this limited sexual role.

     Act II begins with a self-assertion by Chrissy: "I
had this lemonade stand ... at one point in my life. An' I
wanted to have a paper route, but only boys were allowed."
(pp. 39-40) She is beginning to perceive the general oppression of women by men in this statement, and this perception
grows with Chrissy's anger throughout Act II.

     In the second scene of the act, Al leaves her, telling
her, "It just gets old when it's the same woman all the
time, is all," (p. 46) throwing her into a fit of rage in
which she rejects the ideal of womanhood depicted in glamour
magazines as impossible. Guy's offer of friendship temporarily brings her out of this rage, although she makes a mild
claim to her female identity when Guy offers to pass her off
as a man, "Christopher," at the next gay ball. "I ain't no
Christopher, Guy," (p. 55) she tells him, but she does not
get angry again until Guy suggests that he is more attractive
to men than she is. Then she becomes furious, threatening
him with a knife, and then asserting that she can be more
attractive than he, that she can achieve the ideal displayed
in the magazines.

     Chrissy does not express anger only toward Al and

Guy in this act. She tells Susan that she picked up a sol-
dier, led him on, and then dropped him. She also admits
to having spit in the shoe of one of the go-go girls of whose
black boyfriend she is jealous. Finally, she expresses anger toward her parents.

In the last scene of the act, Chrissy is at first angry
only at her mother, who had tried to abort Chrissy. But
when Chrissy confronts her mother, she responds that it was
her father's fault for refusing to use birth control and for
threatening to leave her mother when pregnancy ruined her
appearance. Frustrated and confused, Chrissy ends Act II
saying that she never wants to see either of her parents
again.

In this act, Chrissy's assertions of her own identity
have increased both in number and in intensity, but her anger is diffuse, directed at men and at women, at her parents and at herself, at the ideal she is expected to emulate
and at the suggestion that she might not achieve this ideal.
In most cases, the people at whom she is angry have sought
her out, and her anger is a response to their actions.

In Act III, there is a shift in the pattern of symbolic
action. Chrissy, always approached by others until this
point, finally begins seeking people out: Eric, Susan, and
then her parents. When Eric will not help her to analyze
her handwriting, she finally becomes genuinely angry at him.
He has described her as a poem, and assumes that she has
sought him out to marry him. "I ain't no poem," (p. 81)
she tells him, and yells at him to shut up, warning him that
he is "messing with the universe." (p. 84) When she seeks
Susan late at night and finds her with a man, Chrissy shoves
her away, Chrissy's first act of physical violence in the
play. She goes to her parents with nightmares in which she
does not know if she is a man or a woman, and asks if her
early memories of being sexually molested are true. Her
parents say no, "All that's just something you always wanted,
but not a soul ever did it to you." (p. 91) This encounter
leaves Chrissy momentarily defeated.

The escalating anger and violence in this act drops
off, and Chrissy decides to get married because "I have
come to understand at last how I have lived my life so far
stupid, and people'll never be happy livin' the way I have. I
mean, cruel and mean and selfish. When I didn't even have
a self in me. No ... real self. But I have other virtues."
(p. 97)

But Chrissy has learned too much about her low status, and has built up too much anger for her attempt to lose
herself in marriage to succeed. In the next scene, Chrissy's
anger returns, finally directed towards Al as representative
of men in the socio-sexual hierarchy. "I ain't listenin' to
you any more, Daddyo! Don't you know how I ain't listenin'?
I am a free person--a free goddamn person." (p. 107) She
has made the connection among all men as oppressors in the
hierarchy, and among all women as oppressed. When Al
curses a telephone operator, Chrissy asks, "How come you
gotta call her a bitch? ... That's all women are to you,
ain't it?" (p. 100) She even makes the connection between
women and food as items of consumption for men, when she
tells Al, "I ain't just a hunk of liver for you to pound on!"
(p. 101) But she is wrong in proclaiming her autonomy, as
her beating makes clear.

Chrissy has understood the hierarchy, but she cannot
change it. It is inflexible, "a permanent fixture" as Harold
says of himself, but as is true of the whole unjust patriarchy
he represents. After Al beats her, Chrissy reappears, dancing in a topless joint. The man who introduces her--known
in the script only as THE MAN--tells the audience that "she's
been workin' hard all her life to get this just right." (p. 111)
What Chrissy has finally "gotten right," synecdochally represented by her topless dance, is her place in the immove-
able hierarchy. When Chrissy attempts to assert her freedom, her existence as a full person and not "just a hunk of
liver," she is violently corrected, sacrificed to the existing
order.

THE MAN also says that Chrissy has chosen to appear masked and topless. " 'You got your choice,' she
says when I was talkin' to her. 'What's it gonna be, face
or boobies?' 'Boobies,' we told her. 'Boobies, boobies,
boobies.' " (p. 111) Her choice of costume demonstrates
her own comprehension of her situation. She no longer costumes herself as a bright-eyed, harmless "bunny," a dancer
who expresses a part of herself in her dancing. Instead,
she is costumed as a faceless, sexual object, recognizing
her place in the hierarchy.

Agent:Scene Ratio

In Boom Boom Room, Chrissy is the agent seeking
autonomy in an unjust socio-sexual hierarchy. Thus, the

play is a feminist drama by the definitions employed in this
study. By examining the agent:scene ratio, it is also possible to understand the philosophic school to which this feminist drama is most closely allied.

The conflict between scene and agent is central in
Boom Boom Room. Chrissy's opponent in her increasingly
frustrated struggle for autonomy is not simply an individual,
a group, or a part of her own mentality. Her opponent can
be recognized in every other character's response to her,
combined with her own internal socialization. In other words,
it is the society of the play, the scene, that finally defeats
Chrissy.

This very omnipresence makes the enemy difficult
for Chrissy to discover, much less to overcome. As Chrissy tells Susan, men don't even intend to hurt women, "They
just don't know how not to." (p. 65) Oppression is not the
conscious decision of any individual man, and the men in the
play are society's victims themselves. "Nothin' ever works
out for them," Chrissy says. "They just try and try." (p. 61)
And it is true that the men in the play are pitiable failures,
in and out of prisons and hospitals throughout the play.

Nor are the other women in the play any more in
control of their own situation than the men. Although they
are in competition with Chrissy, they are also as much victims of the hierarchy as she is. When Chrissy resolves to
redeem her life by marrying, the go-go girls are happy for
her, even her former enemies. When she accuses them of
laughing at her romantic aspirations, they reassure her that
they all know how she feels.

All of the oppressors among the men in the play, all
of the competitors among the oppressed class of women, are
also victims of the hierarchy themselves. Even Susan and
Guy, who have reversed their roles in the hierarchy, have
not escaped its limitations. It is not surprising, therefore,
that Chrissy's anger builds slowly, and is at first diffuse.
Only at the end of the play does Chrissy focus on Al, associating him with Harold as representative of the patriarchy.
It is not surprising, either, that such an omnipresent societal system should conquer Chrissy in the end, so that she is
discovered in the last scene dancing with her face masked,
more clearly an impersonal sexual commodity than at the
beginning of the play.

Because scene so thoroughly dominates the play, materialism is the philosophic school to which the play is most
closely allied.   This alliance is evident in the emphasis on
the physical, epitomized in Chrissy's reduction to a faceless
body, a material object without a spirit at the end of the
play.   The determinism associated with materialism is reflected in the play's conclusions: Harold, representative of
the unjust patriarchal system, is indeed a "permanent fixture" in Chrissy's life.   Her recognition of the injustice of
this system and her rebellion against it have resulted in her
being beaten into submission.   The system itself remains
unchanged, and Chrissy is forced to rejoin it, now recognizing her status, but also recognizing her inability to alter it.

Conclusion

In the Boom Boom Room is a feminist drama because
the pattern of symbolic action is one of the agent, Chrissy,
struggling for autonomy.   The clusters of associations in the
play create a scene which is an unjust socio-sexual hierarchy.   Because scene dominates the play, finally defeating
Chrissy in her struggle, the play is allied to the philosophy
of materialism.   Chrissy's individual spirit is reduced in
the final scene to a purely material representation of her as
a faceless, sexual object.

The total inflexibility and final triumph of the unjust
hierarchy in the play make Boom Boom Room a deterministic dramatic statement.   The play is a moving but despairing
portrayal of woman as object in a rigid, patriarchal society.

Notes

1.   New York Times, 24 November 1973, p. 22.

2.   David Rabe, introduction to The Basic Training of Pavlo
      Hummel and Sticks and Bones (New York: Viking
      Press, 1973), p. xxv.

3.   Ibid.

4.   Ibid.

5.   Stanley Kauffmann, "Stanley Kauffmann on Theater," New
      Republic, December 1, 1973, p. 22.

6.   New York Times, 24 November 1973, p. 22.

7.   Review of In the Boom Boom Room, New York Times,
     5 December 1974, p. 55.

8.   David Rabe, interview in New York Times, 12 May
     1976, p. 34.

9.   David Rabe, interview in New York Times, 24 Novem-
     ber 1973, p. 22.

10. David Rabe, interview in New York Times, 25 April
     1976, sec. 2, p. 12.

11. Walter Kerr, "David Rabe's 'House' Is Not a Home,"
     New York Times, 2 May 1976, sec. 2, p. 5.

12. David Rabe, In the Boom Boom Room (New York: Al-
     fred A. Knopf, 1975), p. 97. Subsequent page ref-
     erences to In the Boom Boom Room in this chapter
     will be in parentheses following the quote in the text.

13. This quote also makes it clear that Chrissy's sexuality
     has some power in Eric's mind. But it is a "mys-
     terious" power, the veiled power of the "other."
     Consequently, it does not give Chrissy the ability to
     make herself subject, rather than object, to become
     autonomous.

Chapter 4

WINE IN THE WILDERNESS

Introduction

Wine in the Wilderness* by Alice Childress shows a black woman's assertion of her autonomy in an "educated" black culture striving to imitate the white patriarchy. The associational clusters in the play reveal a false ideal of subservient, glamorous black womanhood, opposed to another false picture of contemporary black women as domineering matriarchs. The associational cluster surrounding Tommy, the protagonist, opposes both of these with an image of the self-reliant black woman seeking equality with men. Tommy's symbolic actions are assertions of her autonomy, at first unconscious expressions of her character, and finally, in the climactic scene, a conscious rejection of the false ideals held by the other characters.

Because the white hierarchical structure has not been fully adopted by the black culture in the play, it is possible for Tommy to transcend the limitations of such a hierarchy herself, and to convert the society around her to an ideal of equality and mutual respect. The philosophic conclusions of the play are idealistic. Tommy's individual spirit overcomes the societal determinants in the play, making it an optimistic statement of the feminist impulse.

Biography

Alice Childress is the author of Florence, Gold Thru the Trees, Just a Little Simple (an adaptation of Langston Hughes's Simple Speaks His Mind), Trouble in Mind, "Mojo," "String," and Wedding Band. Trouble in Mind won an Obie

---

*Wine in the Wilderness, by Alice Childress in Plays By and About Women, ed. by Victoria Sullivan and James Hatch (New York: Random House, 1974). Quotes from this play reprinted by permission.

award in 1955-56 and was produced twice by the BBC in London. Wedding Band was first produced at the University of Michigan as its Professional Theater Production of 1966 with Ruby Dee, Abbey Lincoln, and Jack Harkins. In 1972, Joseph Papp produced it off Broadway and then produced the teleplay on ABC National Network.

Abbey Lincoln played the leading role in the WGBH production for Boston television of Wine in the Wilderness. This production was part of a series by black authors aired in 1969.

In 1971, Childress edited a book of scenes for black actors, in which she commented on the work of black playwrights:

> Often we have heard complaints about the one theme used most by Black writers, freedom. But seldom are writers of any race able to write outside of their own experience. Black experience means living a segregated and very special existence. There may be a few who were raised within a white experience and so are able to write best in this vein, but it is indeed rare.[1]

In collaboration with her husband, Nathan Woodard, Childress has completed a musical, "Sea Island Song," which played schools and institutions throughout South Carolina. They also wrote a musical, "A King Remembered," the story of Martin Luther King's Montgomery bus boycott. It was presented by Performing Arts Repertory Theatre Foundation and toured for three seasons. Childress has written a children's book, A Hero Ain't Nothin' but a Sandwich, and, in 1975, two children's plays, When the Rattlesnake Sounds and "Let's Hear It for the Queen." A film version of Hero was recently released. "String" is in rehearsal for K. C. E. T. "Visions" series at this writing.

Childress was one of a group of black playwrights asked by the New York Times in 1969 whether it is possible for black and white artists to work together in the theatre. She responded:

> The time is over for asking or even demanding human rights, in or out of the theater. We no longer ask for manhood or womanhood or dignity; all we can do is express what we have to the de-

gree that we have it. All whites aren't good or
bad, the same goes for blacks--but this equalizes
nothing. The whole racism mess is based upon
the action of white supremacist thought and deed.
    In the past forty years only eighteen plays by
black writers have been presented on Broadway.
Soon we may have to read our works on the side-
walks of inner city and "mainstream" Broadway.
Time is up. I've a play to write that may never
be seen by any audience anywhere, but I do my
thing. Who has ears to hear, hear ... all others,
later. [2]

Plot Summary

    Wine in the Wilderness is set in the apartment of a
black artist, Bill, just after a riot. His neighbors Cynthia
and Sonny-man bring him a model, a young woman they have
just met in a bar while waiting out the riot. The woman,
Tomorrow Marie, or Tommy, is to model the third panel
of a triptych Bill is painting on the subject of black womanhood.

    Bill describes the triptych to Oldtimer, another neigh-
bor, before the others arrive. One panel shows an innocent
little black girl, and another shows the ideal: a cold, perfect beauty in African garb. She is the centerpiece, the
"Wine in the Wilderness." Tommy is to be a contrast to
her:

            The lost woman ... what the society has made
            out of our women. She's as far from my African
            queen as a woman can get and still be female,
            she's as close to the bottom as you can get with-
            out crackin' up ... she's ignorant, unfeminine,
            coarse, rude ... vulgar ... a poor dumb chick
            that's had her behind kicked until it's numb ... and
            the sad part is ... she ain't together, you know,
            ... there's no hope for her. [3]

    Tommy arrives with Cynthia and Sonny-man, believing
that they are introducing her to Bill in hopes of a romance
between the two. When the men leave to get Tommy some
Chinese food, she tells Cynthia that she would like to be
married and that she is attracted to Bill. Cynthia's advice
is to stop wearing a wig, and to be less brash and self-

sufficient. "Expect more. Learn to let men open doors for
you...." Tommy answers, "What if I'm standin' there and
they don't open it?" (p. 401) Cynthia tries to warn Tommy
not to expect romance.

When the men return, Cynthia, Sonny-man, and Oldtimer go home. The Chinese restaurant has been destroyed
in the riot, so Bill has brought Tommy a frankfurter and an
orange drink instead. Tommy is somewhat insulted, but she
resigns herself to the supper. While trying to model and
eat at the same time, she spills her orange drink on her
dress. Bill gives her an African throw to wear instead.
While she is changing, she overhears Bill on the phone, describing the "Wine in the Wilderness" painting. She believes
that he is describing her, and comes out in the wrap without
her wig, relaxed and confident that he likes her. Because
of her change in mood and costume, she is more attractive
to Bill, and they end by spending the night together.

The next morning, Oldtimer returns and accidentally
reveals that Tommy was to be the "messed-up chick" in the
triptych. Cynthia and Sonny-man arrive, and Tommy de-
nounces all of them, saying that they pretend to support
their own people, but actually hate them, as evidenced by
their treatment of her. As she is about to leave, Bill, who
has been apologizing, is inspired to begin a new triptych.
This one will show Oldtimer on one side as the Negro's
past, and Sonny-man and Cynthia on the other as the young
man and woman of the more optimistic present. In the center, he persuades Tommy to stay and model the hope of the
future, herself, Tomorrow Marie.

Associational Clusters

In the first scene of Wine in the Wilderness, two of
the important clusters of associations in the play make their
first appearances. Bill establishes the cluster of associations defining his ideal black woman, and the one defining
her opposite, the "nothing" black woman, in this scene.

Before a word is spoken, the audience can tell from
the setting that Bill has a taste for the exotic. According
to the stage directions, "The room is obviously black dominated, pieces of sculpture, wall hangings, paintings." It also
"reflects an interest in other darker peoples of the world....
A Chinese incense-burner Buddha, an American Indian feath-

ered war helmet, a Mexican serape, a Japanese fan, a West
Indian travel poster." (p. 383) Bill's ideal woman, the
"Wine in the Wilderness" painting, shares the exotic quality
of his furnishings:

> Mother Africa, regal, black womanhood in her
> noblest form.... This Abyssinian maiden is
> paradise, ... She's the Sudan, the Congo River,
> the Egyptian Pyramids ... Her thighs are African
> Mahogany ... she speaks and her words pour forth
> sparkling clear as the waters ... Victoria Falls.
> (pp. 387-388)

These images, with the set decorations, form a cluster of
associations around exotic, foreign beauty.

The second cluster of associations in this scene forms
around the opposite of this ideal, the "lost woman." Her
associations are with "grass roots." She is "a back country
chick right outta the wilds of Mississippi, ... but she ain'
never been near there. Born in Harlem, raised right here
in Harlem, ... but back country." (p. 388) She is "ignorant, unfeminine, coarse, rude ... vulgar." (p. 388) This
cluster of associations is the opposite of the first, negative
rather than positive, and familiar rather than exotic.

Oldtimer, hearing the first cluster of associations,
comments that Victoria Falls is a pretty name for a woman.
So foreign are the associations clustering around Bill's ideal
black woman that they are laughably unfamiliar to an unedu-
cated American black like Oldtimer. In contrast, when Oldtimer hears the description of "the lost woman" later in this
scene, he recognizes it at once, and says, "Oh, man, you
talkin' 'bout my first wife." (p. 388) The positive qualities
in Bill's triptych are unrecognizable to a black man off the
street, but the negative qualities are a completely familiar
critique of black women. Although this is evident to the
audience from Oldtimer's reactions in the first scene, it
takes Bill the rest of the play to reach this awareness.

In the last scene, Tommy tells him:

> If a black somebody is in a history book, or
> printed on a pitcher, or drawed on a paintin', ...
> or if they're a statue, ... dead, and outta the
> way, and can't talk back, then you dig 'em and
> full-a so much-a damn admiration and talk 'bout

"our" history.   But when you run into us livin'
and breathin' ones, with the life's blood still
pumpin' through us, ... then you comin' on 'bout
how we ain' never together.   You hate us, that's
what." (p. 417)

And the stage directions tell us that Bill is "stung to the
heart" by this distinction between the associations surrounding his ideal, and those surrounding his view of real black
women.

When Tommy and Cynthia discuss Bill, the cluster
of associations around his ideal grows.   Cynthia says that
in order to please Bill, Tommy should stop wearing her wig.
She should also "let him do the talking.   Learn to listen.
Stay in the background a little.   Ask his opinion ... 'What
do you think, Bill?' " (p. 400)   This description fits very
well with Bill's analysis of what is wrong with black women
in a later scene.   "Our women don't know a damn thing
'bout bein' feminine.   Give in sometime." (p. 406)   The
ideal black woman, he says, should "throw them suppers together, keep your husband happy, raise the kids." (p. 405)

The cluster surrounding Bill's ideal of womanhood,
then, includes not only exotic beauty but subservience to
men.   Cynthia and Bill envision a socio-sexual hierarchy in
which men are dominant.   Tommy, however, when she hears
Cynthia's suggestions, says, "Mmmmm.   'Oh, hooty, hooty,
hoo'," a comment she has made a few lines earlier in reference to white men.   "The dullest people in the world.   The
way they talk ... 'Oh, hooty, hooty, hoo' ... break it down
for me to A, B, C's." (p. 400)   Tommy is correct in associating Cynthia's description with white men.   The behavior
that Cynthia says will please Bill is the behavior demanded
of women in the white patriarchal society.

According to Cynthia, Tommy's problem is having
been raised in a matriarchal society which has robbed black
men of their manhood.   In other words, Cynthia is describing a reversal of the socio-sexual hierarchy in which women
are dominant.   Tommy rejects this idea, saying that women
did not rule in her family because: "We didn't have nothin'
to rule over, not a pot nor a window." (p. 399)   When Cynthia tells Tommy to give the black man his manhood, Tommy answers, "I didn't take it from him, how I'm gonna give
it back?" (p. 399)

To these two choices, the cluster of associations surrounding a subservient role for women in imitation of white
patriarchy or the cluster surrounding a black matriarchy of
"lost women," Tommy adds a third alternative: equal roles
for women and men.   Describing her dream to Cynthia, Tommy says that she is looking for a man "to meet me halfway."
(p. 397)   She does not expect him to support her; rather
"the both of you gotta pull together.   That way you accomplish." (p. 397)   She hopes for companionship: "Somebody
in my corner.   Not to wake up by myself in the mornin' and
face this world all alone." (p. 398)   The third cluster of
associations, defining Tommy's ideal, begins to form in this
scene.

The three clusters of associations--around Bill's exotic
ideal, around the "lost," matriarchal, black woman, and
around Tommy, the woman seeking an equal relationship--
continue to develop in subsequent scenes.   In Tommy's next
scene with Bill, the cluster of associations surrounding his
ideal grows to include Afro-American history.   He has pictures on his wall of Frederick Douglass and John Brown,
and tells Tommy about other figures in black history with
whom she is not familiar.   But he discourages her questions
about them, saying, "Trouble with our women, ... they all
wanta be great brains.   Leave somethin' for a man to do."
(p. 405)   Although his ideal includes heroic men and women
in history, it also includes ignorant women in the present
day, allowing their men intellectual superiority.

Tommy also finds a picture on his wall of a blonde,
blue-eyed model who, Bill says, could sit on her long, silky
hair.   Tommy responds bitterly, saying that it is this attitude that forces her to wear a wig, " 'cause you and those
like you go for long, silky hair, and this is the only way I
can have some without burnin' my mother-grabbin' brains
out." (p. 408)   Although Bill claims that his ideal is black,
it is in fact an imitation of the white ideal of womanhood
symbolized by the blonde model: an ornamental, subservient
woman without intellectual independence.

Tommy counters this false ideal when, later in the
same scene, she overhears Bill describing his painting and
believes that he is in love with her.   Confident of his appre-
ciation, she appears without the wig symbolic of the false
ideal of beauty.   In an effective reversal of Bill's history
lesson, Tommy reveals her own local history, more personal
and touching than Bill's version, and showing honest pride:

> I had a uncle who was an "Elk," ... a member
> of "The Improved Benevolent Protective Order of
> Elks of the World": "The Henry Lincoln Johnson
> Lodge." You know, the white "Elks" are called
> "The Benevolent Protective Order of Elks" but the
> black "Elks are called "The Improved Benevolent
> Protective Order of Elks of the World." That's
> because the black "Elks" got the copyright first
> but the white "Elks" took us to court about it to
> keep us from usin' the name. Over fifteen hun-
> dred black folk went to jail for wearin' the "Elk"
> emblem on their coat lapel. Years ago, ... that's
> what you call history." (p. 410)

Tommy's history, in contrast to Bill's, is filled with "real"
people, often members of her own family, and their small
but real accomplishments--winning a scholarship in a speech
contest, for instance, or tracing the family history back to
slaves from Sweetwater Springs, Virginia. She reveals her
personality in her history and in preferences such as pink
roses for corsages and four o'clocks for bush flowers.

Bill's negative associations with this kind of local,
recent history, part of the cluster surrounding the "lost
woman," appear in his description of his own family:

> Everybody in my family worked for the Post Of-
> fice. They bought a house in Jamaica, Long Is-
> land. Everybody on that block bought an aluminum
> screen door with a duck on it, ... or was it a
> swan? I guess that makes my favorite flower
> crab grass and hedges." (p. 411)

In Bill's mind, only the exotic is positive; the familiar is always vulgar, not "together."

The three clusters of associations finally conflict
directly in the last scene when Tommy discovers that she is
not "Wine in the Wilderness" to Bill, but a model for the
"messed-up chick" in his triptych. Her wig figures symbolically once more, when Tommy tells Cynthia that Tommy
does, indeed, have to wear a wig: "To soften the blow when
yall go upside-a my head with a baseball bat." (p. 416) In
other words, Tommy needs the wig, which she had felt safe
in removing, as a defense against the false ideal of beauty.

Tommy makes the distinction between Bill's positive,

exotic ideal and his negative view of real black women explicit in this final scene: "Ain't a-one-a us you like that's
alive and walkin' by you on the street ... you don't like
flesh and blood niggers." (p. 416) It is not the screen doors
with ducks on them that offended him in his childhood, she
says: "You didn't like who was livin' behind them screen
doors. Phoney Nigger!" (p. 417)

Bill's ideal is false not only because it is unrealistic-
ally exotic and based on white values, but also because it
objectifies the black woman--makes an "other" of her just
as the white society does of white women. In the final
scene, Tommy asserts her autonomy, her ability to be subject rather than object, to be a "real," contemporary black
woman who is admirable:

> Bill, I don't have to wait for anybody's by-your-
> leave to be a "Wine in the Wilderness" woman.
> I can be it if I wanta, ... and I am. I am. I
> am. I'm not the one you made up and painted,
> the very pretty lady who can't talk back, ... but
> I'm "Wine in the Wilderness" ... alive and kickin'
> me ... Tomorrow Marie, cussin' and fightin' and
> lookin' out for my damn self 'cause ain' nobody
> else 'round to do it, dontcha know. (p. 420)

The falsity of Bill's ideal finally becomes clear to him. He
rejects the exotic "other," the black queen he has imagined.
"She's not it at all, Tommy, This chick on the canvas, ...
nothin' but accessories, a dream I dreamed up outta the junk
of my mind. You are ... the real beautiful people." (p. 420)
The painting, and Tommy, are explicitly identified as representative at the end of the play.

In fact, each of the associational clusters has elements
on each of the three levels distinguished by Burke: the sensory, the familial, and the abstract. On the sensory level
are the physical descriptions of the "Wine in the Wilderness"
painting, of the planned painting of the "lost woman," and of
Tommy when she appears as her natural self in an African
throw, without her wig. On the familial level, the "Wine
in the Wilderness" woman is "Mother Africa" and the "lost
woman" is the domineering matriarch destroying her family.
Tommy is associated with the positive, familial images of
her family history.

On the abstract level, all three clusters operate as

symbolic representations of black womanhood. The "Wine
in the Wilderness" painting represents the false ideal of exotic
beauty and subservience in imitation of the white socio-sexual
hierarchy. The "lost woman" represents the black matriarchy, a reversed socio-sexual hierarchy supposedly destroying
black society. And Tommy represents the true societal ideal,
autonomous and equal women and men.

Pattern of Symbolic Action

Tommy's assertions of her own autonomy and pride
in her race make up the pattern of symbolic action of the
play. From the beginning, Tommy displays these qualities
unconsciously in her behavior. By asking Oldtimer's real
name, something his friends have never bothered to do, she
shows respect for another black person. "I'll call you Oldtimer like the rest but I like to know who I'm meetin'," she
says. (p. 391) Later in this scene, Tommy explains that,
although she could keep house for a white family on Park
Avenue, she prefers to work in a factory and live among her
black friends in Harlem. In her scene with Cynthia, Tommy
says that she never gave up dating white men as Cynthia did.
"I never had none to give up," she says. "I'm not soundin'
on you. White folks, nothin' happens when I look at 'em.
I don't hate 'em, don't love 'em, ... just nothin' shakes
a-tall. The dullest people in the world." (p. 400) Throughout the play, Tommy shows more respect and love for her
own race than the others do, just as she shows respect for
herself.

Tommy tells Cynthia that she would like to marry because she is lonely, but "I don't want any and everybody.
What I want with a no-good piece-a nothin'?" (p. 397) Tommy
has too much self-respect to marry someone she does not
love and admire. Later in the play, she demonstrates this
attitude again, when Bill brings her a frankfurter instead of
Chinese food. She likes Bill very much, as she has just
told Cynthia. But her liking and her hopes of marriage
don't stop her from objecting to this supper. "You brought
me a frank-footer? That's what you think a-me, a frank-
footer?" Bill says that kings and queens eat frankfurters,
but Tommy is not put off. "If a queen sent you out to buy
her a bucket-a Foo-yung, you wouldn't come back with no
lonely-ass frank-footer," (p. 402) she says.

Tommy's account of her family history further dem-

onstrates her respect for herself and her race. And she
consistently rejects Cynthia's and Bill's suggestions that she
be more subservient, usually on grounds of common sense.
When Cynthia suggests that she not chase Bill, "at least
don't let it look that way. Let him pursue you," Tommy
answers, "What if he won't? Men don't chase me much,
not the kind I like." (p. 400) When Cynthia tells Tommy
that black women "do for ourselves too much," Tommy answers, "If I don't, who's gonna do for me?" (p. 399) But
to Bill's suggestion that she should "keep your husband happy, raise the kids," she responds, "Bein' married and havin'
a family might be good for your people as a race, but I was
thinkin' 'bout myself a little." (p. 406)

This statement demonstrates the unconscious quality
of Tommy's assertions of autonomy. She seems to suggest
that assertiveness and "thinking about herself" might be
wrong, and that the subservient, objectified ideal held up by
Cynthia and Bill might be more beneficial to her race. The
turning point in the pattern of symbolic action comes when
Tommy decides that she is right in asserting her autonomy.

Up until the point of her decision, the other characters have attempted to reprimand and correct Tommy's assertions of her autonomy. Tommy, while she has not backed
down, has admitted that the others probably know more about
correct behavior than she does. When Bill tells her to say
"Afro-Americans," not "niggers," she does, at least for a
while. She tells Cynthia: "If there's somethin' wrong that I
can change, I'm ready to do it. Eighth grade, that's all I
had of school. You a social worker, I know that mean college." (p. 398) Examining Bill's books and pictures on
black history, Tommy says, "This room is full-a things I
don't know nothin' about. How'll I get to know?" (p. 405)
All of these comments indicate Tommy's acceptance of her
own inferiority, and the unconscious quality of her own attitude of self-respect.

The turning point in the pattern of symbolic action
comes when Tommy discovers that she was to model for the
"messed-up chick" in the triptych. All of Tommy's former
assertions of autonomy and all of the reproofs she accepted
from Cynthia and Bill appear in a new light to her at that
point. She throws Cynthia's advice on wigs back in her face
in this scene. She corrects Sonny-man for calling her "the
sister": "If you feelin' so brotherly why don't you say 'my'
sister? Ain't no we-ness in your talk. 'The' Afro-American,

'the' black man, there's no we-ness in you. Who you think
you are?" (p. 417) She tells Oldtimer: "You their fool too.
'Til I got here they didn't even know your damn name." (p.
416) She rejects Bill's knowledge of Afro-American history,
knocking his books to the floor and saying, "There's something inside-a me that says I ain' suppose to let nobody play
me cheap. Don't care how much they know!" (p. 416) And
she insists on calling Bill a nigger over his protests that
she is using the word incorrectly because, he says, "A nigger
is a low, degraded person, any low degraded person." He
looks it up in the dictionary to prove his point, and discovers
that the definition is: "A Negro ... a member of any dark-
skinned people." (p. 418)

All of this only re-affirms what has already become
clear to the audience: that Tommy is the truly autonomous
individual, and Bill, Sonny-man and Cynthia are striving for
a false ideal imitative of the white patriarchy, despite their
education and sophistication. But the scene is important because it is the point in the play at which this distinction finally reaches Tommy's consciousness.

Tommy's earlier belief in the others' superior education and her fear that her assertiveness is not for the good
of the race are laid to rest in this scene. She regrets her
previous assumption of her own inferiority: "Trouble is I
was Tommin' to you, to all of you, ... 'Oh, maybe they
gon' like me.' ... I was your fool, thinkin' writers and
painters know more'n me, that maybe a little bit of you would
rub off on me." (p. 416)

Seeing the falsity of their ideal--the cluster of associations surrounding the "Wine in the Wilderness" painting--
she asserts that the elements of this ideal are just "accessories": "Somethin' you add on or take off. The real thing
is takin' place on the inside ... that's where the action is.
That's 'Wine in the Wilderness,' ... a woman that's a real
one and a good one. And yall just better believe I'm it."
(p. 420) And she starts for the door, having become fully
aware of her own autonomy.

This new awareness is the significant change in motivation in the play. Tommy realizes that it is a change, and
tells the others, "I hate to do it but I have to thank you
'cause I'm walkin' out with much more than I brought in."
(p. 419) She is walking out with a new awareness of her own
strength, of her own power to assert her autonomy, something she has done unconsciously throughout the play.

Agent:Scene Ratio

Because Wine in the Wilderness shows a female protagonist, Tommy, asserting her autonomy in opposition to an
unjust socio-sexual hierarchy, the play can be considered a
feminist drama.   Analysis of the agent-scene ratio reveals
the play's affinity to a particular philosophic school: idealism.   Because Tommy's achievement of autonomy is emphasized, the play is idealistic, showing the triumph of the individual spirit.

The depiction of scene, the unjust socio-sexual hierarchy, is unusual in Wine in the Wilderness.   The socio-
sexual hierarchy in which man is "mounter" and woman is
"mounted" is not the norm in the society of the play, but
rather is the ideal toward which the characters believe they
should strive.   The problem with the black sub-culture, Bill
and Cynthia believe, is that it is a matriarchy in which woman is mounter, thereby depriving black men of their mascu-
line role.

But Tommy disagrees with this depiction of her society.   Women do not rule in the black society; rather, they
are the most oppressed members of the oppressed black caste.
Her own mother "ruled" in the home only because her father
deserted the family: "My pappa picked hisself up and run off
with some finger-poppin' woman and we never hear another
word 'til ten, twelve years later when a undertaker call up
and ask if Mama wanta claim his body." (p. 399)   If black
women are strong, Tommy maintains that it is because they
have had to be self-sufficient.

Because black women have been forced to be self-
sufficient, and because black men have been oppressed, the
black culture has not succeeded in imitating thoroughly the
socio-sexual hierarchy of white society.   As a result, it is
possible for Tommy to assert her autonomy within this sub-
culture, and to seek a relationship of equality outside of either
a patriarchal or a matriarchal structure.

In doing so, she is at first opposed by the scene, the
"educated" element of black society which maintains that a
patriarchy is the race's hope of the future, and which holds
up as ideal the glamorous but subservient, objectified "Wine
in the Wilderness" woman.   Finally, however, Tommy's assertion of her own individuality is revealed as a more sincere
black pride, a more perfect ideal than Bill's painting or
Cynthia's image of the patriarchal society.

According to Burke, if the agent's achievement is featured in a play, the play is idealistic. In an idealistic play, spirit triumphs over matter; the individual transcends societal limitations. In Wine in the Wilderness, Tommy's individual spirit transcends the hierarchical view of society formerly held by the other characters.

In the last scene of the play, Bill replaces the "Wine in the Wilderness" painting with a picture of Tommy, thus symbolically replacing the objectified, subservient image of black womanhood with Tommy, the autonomous subject. By speaking up for herself, Tommy has not only gained a new consciousness of her own individual spirit, but she has converted the society around her to a new ideal. Bill summarizes what her self-reliance and pride represent as an ideal for their race:

> Look at Tomorrow. She came through the biggest riot of all, ... somethin' called "Slavery," and she's even comin' through the "now" scene, ... folks laughin' at her, even her own folks laughin' at her. And look how ... with her head high up like she's poppin' her fingers at the world. (Takes up charcoal pencil and tears old page off sketch pad so he can make a fresh drawing) Aw, let me put it down, Tommy. "Wine in the Wilderness," you gotta let me put it down so all the little boys and girls can look up and see you on the wall. And you know what they're gonna say? "Hey, don't she look like somebody we know?" (p. 421)

Tommy is "somebody we know," an individual whose spirit triumphs over matter, making the play an idealistic, feminist drama.

Conclusion

Because Wine in the Wilderness depicts a female protagonist asserting her autonomy in opposition to an unjust socio-sexual hierarchy, it is a feminist drama. The associational clusters in the play show a false ideal of subservient black womanhood, a negative cluster describing the supposed black matriarch, and a cluster describing the truly autonomous, individual black woman seeking equality. The pattern of symbolic action is one of Tommy's repeated assertions of her autonomy, at first unconscious and made from an assump-

tion of inferiority. At the turning point in the play's motivation, Tommy becomes aware of her own self-worth, and
converts the society of the play to her values. Agent dominates in this drama, in which Tommy's individual spirit
transcends the false ideal of a patriarchal socio-sexual hierarchy. The play is an idealistic, optimistic statement of the
feminist impulse.

Notes

1. Alice Childress, ed., Black Scenes (New York: Double-
    day and Company, 1971), p. xi.

2. Alice Childress, interview in New York Times, 2 Febru-
    ary 1969, sec. 2, p. 1.

3. Alice Childress, Wine in the Wilderness in Plays By and
    About Women, eds. Victoria Sullivan and James Hatch
    (New York: Random House, 1974), p. 388. Subse-
    quent page references to Wine in the Wilderness are
    in parentheses following the quote in the text.

Chapter 5

BIRTH AND AFTER BIRTH

Introduction

Honor Moore, discussing the plays anthologized in
The New Women's Theatre, uses the term "feminist" as if it
were synonymous with "concerning women." A play is feminist, she implies, if women can identify with its characters
and situations, if they feel "taken in, included" by their experiences in the theatre.[1] She has chosen to anthologize
plays that fit this criterion, a criterion that many casual
readers and audience members would accept as defining feminist drama.

Birth and After Birth* by Tina Howe, published in
Moore's anthology, fits her suggested definition easily. The
play examines a situation with which contemporary women can
readily identify: that of the American nuclear family. In its
humorous depiction of the Apple family and their attempt to
convert their professional friends to family life, the play
reveals the limitations such a life places upon father, mother,
and child. In the claustrophobic atmosphere of their home,
the father is like an insecure child himself in his behavior,
the mother is tired and old before her time, and the son is
spoiled and egotistical from too much attention. Nevertheless, the play ends with a tableau of the three of them fro-
zen in "an endless embrace."

Because Birth and After Birth is a play that many
people, like Moore, would consider feminist, it provides an
interesting subject for analysis by the definitions employed in
this study. Examination of the play's associational clusters
will reveal the kind of hierarchy on which the play's society
is based. Its pattern of symbolic action will show what goal
the agent pursues. If the goal, or purpose, is autonomy,

---

*Birth and After Birth, by Tina Howe in The New Women's
Theatre, ed. by Honor Moore. (New York: Random House,
1977). Quotes from this play reprinted by permission.

pursued against the opposition of an unjust socio-sexual hierarchy, then the play can be considered feminist in its rhetorical motive, by somewhat more exacting standards than Moore
employs. But if the play does not fit this definition, the
method of analysis will reveal what the play's rhetorical motive is, and comparing the play with the definition should elucidate both the play and the definition itself.

   The clusters of associations in Birth and After Birth
do not, in fact, reveal a hierarchy which is sexually based,
nor is the pattern of symbolic action an agent's struggle for
autonomy. For this very reason, combined with Birth and
After Birth's obvious relevance to women's concerns, the
analysis of this play has been included as a demonstration
in the present study. The definitions employed here can be
used, not only to group plays with a feminist rhetorical motive, but to distinguish between those plays and plays that
are in some ways similar, but have a different rhetorical
motive.

Biography

   Tina Howe wrote her first play, a one-act, while a
senior at Sarah Lawrence College, where it was directed by
her friend Jane Alexander, now an actress. She went on to
teach high school in Maine and then in Wisconsin: "I taught
English, and they were always looking for someone to run
the dramatics department--I would agree to do it on the condition that I could produce my own plays.... That's how I
learned what worked and what didn't work--if you can keep
the attention of an audience of teenagers, then it's working...."[2]

   Her first full length play to be produced was The
Nest, co-produced off Broadway in 1970 by Anne McIntosh,
Thayer Burch, and Honor Moore. Honor Moore described
the play as "a comic surreal treatment of the lives of three
archetypal female roommates whose apartment on the 150th
floor of an anonymous building has 'a view of heaven.' "[3]
According to Moore, the play was not well received by critics because it expressed a "female vision."

   A later play by Howe, Museum, was produced in 1976
at the Los Angeles Actors' Theatre and at the Public Theatre
in New York. Birth and After Birth was first produced as a
workshop at the Gotham Art Theatre in New York City in 1974,
with Howe directing. Howe said of the play:

> I wrote Birth and After Birth out of my own
> experience, but also out of the experience of
> women I knew where I lived in the country.
> I was different because I always had my writing.
> I wrote this play for the suburban woman with
> no exit from her kitchen and a four-year-old
> seven feet tall. [4]

The play would, she hoped, tell another side of family life:
"As a mother, you experience moments of excruciating tenderness and love, but there is also great savagery--family
life has been over-romanticized; the savagery has not been
seen enough in the theatre and in movies...."[5]

Howe lives in New York with her husband and two
children. Her ambition, she says, "is to get a thousand
people in a dark room laughing themselves nearly to death,
drenched in tears, rolling in the aisles, ambulances rushing
to theatre doors."[6]

Plot Summary

Birth and After Birth opens in Sandy and Bill Apple's
kitchen-playroom at dawn on the fourth birthday of their son,
Nicky. The Apples are decorating the house and wrapping
presents. Suddenly Nicky, who is to be played by an adult,
bursts in, shouting, "Where's my presents? Where's my
presents?"[7] Nicky tears through his gifts while Sandy futilely tries to persuade him to open the cards first. Bill is
making a home movie for the occasion, and urges Nicky to
unwrap and play with his toys for the camera.

Sandy notices that there is sand in her hair, and that
she keeps smelling the sea at low tide, although they are
hundreds of miles from the ocean. Meanwhile, Bill is still
trying to get footage on the movie camera, since he can have
the film developed the same day and show it to their guests
for the evening, Sandy's cousins, Jeffrey and Mia Freed.

Sandy and Nicky play a game with the masks he has
gotten as gifts, in which Nicky is a baby again and Sandy is
his mommy. While they are playing, Bill reads her a letter
he has received through his office mail, criticizing his recent work. Sandy pays no attention to him, and Bill eventually gets angry and leaves the room.

Nicky begins demanding grape juice, which Sandy will

not give him. Finally she slaps him. He makes a strangled
sound and falls in an apparent faint. Sandy panics and calls
Bill. They walk Nicky around, feed him ice, get out the
flashlight and the tourniquet, and finally apply artificial res-
piration. Nicky wakes up.

Bill and Sandy discuss the Freeds, who are anthro-
pologists specializing in the study of primitive children.
Sandy hopes that Jeff and Mia will see how happy the Apples
are, and will want children themselves. Nicky keeps interrupting them to ask if he can make his birthday wish. Finally, Nicky leaves the room and Sandy and Bill reminisce
about their own birthday parties when they were children.
They are interrupted by Nicky, who reappears in his mother's
underwear, demanding grape juice with ice. When he is given
warm juice, he throws the glass down and is sent to his room.
Sandy and Bill tell him that there will be no birthday party.

As Act II begins, the Apples are waiting for the Freeds
to start the party. The Freeds arrive and begin telling fab-
ulous stories of primitive children who at age four are "blind-
folded and led into a swamp to bring back the body of a mud
turtle for a tribal feast," (p. 143) or who "skin a six-hundred-
pound zebra and eat the pelt!" (p. 144) In response, Nicky
offers his own accomplishments: writing his name and pull-
ing his mother in his new wagon.

Jeff and Mia give their present to Nicky, a slide pro-
jector and slides of the primitive children they have met.
They tell about the most remarkable tribe they studied, the
Whan See. While they are talking, "NICKY picks up a cello
and begins playing the Bach unaccompanied cello suites."
(p. 161) The Whan See are a gentle, beautiful tribe. But
they have one flaw, which Mia describes. When a Whan See
woman gives birth, the child is immediately forced back into
the womb and is then born again, over and over. Describing
this practice, Mia starts to cry. Sandy tries to reassure
her that childbirth is nothing to fear.

The Apples go into a charade of childbirth with Mia
as the mother, despite her protests. Finally, Mia passes
out. Jeff assures them that Mia faints all the time. They
prop her up at the table for birthday cake, and Nicky finally
makes his birthday wish: for a brother.

Jeff decides to leave--before Bill has shown his mo-
vie--and as soon as he starts to go, Mia wakes up. Bill

decides to show his movie without them, and as he does, Sandy
says, "Four years ago today, Nicky, you made us the happiest
family in the world." (p. 187)

Associational Clusters

Unlike the plays discussed in earlier chapters, Birth
and After Birth's associational clusters do not establish a hierarchy in which men are above women. Rather, the associational clusters in the play distinguish the couple with a child
from the couple without. The familial is the most significant
of Burke's three levels of meaning in this play, because the
contrast between the Apples and the Freeds is, most importantly, in the kind of family life they are living. But this
same contrast is also reflected on the sensory level. The
Apples are associated with food, with animals, with eating
one's young, all in a cluster revolving around Nicky. They
are also associated with failure, decay, and old age. The
Freeds are associated with parallel but contrasting associations on the sensory level. On the abstract level are the
Apples' general statements on family life, which depict the
Apples and the Freeds as representative of two kinds of societal family unit.

The Apples' first cluster of sensory associations includes Sandy's description of Nicky when he was a baby as
"a little blue trout" (p. 115) with skinny arms like "french-
fried potatoes," (p. 116) a description that makes Nicky sound
as though he were edible. All of Nicky's conflicts with his
parents are over food: raisins or grape juice. Nicky's
games with his parents involve making animal noises or playing Rabbit Says, a game like Simon Says in which Nicky is
the Rabbit. When Nicky is recovering from his fainting fit,
he and his parents play a game of pretending that he is Rabbit Boy, "a champion of rabbits in distress." (p. 123) Bill
says that Nicky sounds like some "sea animal, ... some
squid or something" (p. 108) when he sucks his thumb. Hearing that the Whan See have a flaw, Bill guesses that they
must eat their young, although nothing the Freeds have said
about them suggests this.

Jeff and Mia are also associated with children and
food, but in a contrasting cluster of sensory associations.
Although references to animals and to eating are frequent in
their stories, the natives never seem to eat what our culture considers food. Instead, they eat zebra pelts or pre-

pare banquets of treebark or mud turtles. The Whan See
are described in terms of food. They are said to smell of
cinnamon and to have pink eyes like strawberry parfait. The
Freeds are associated with animals too, but in exotic situations. They have known children who can nurse dead goats
back to life, for instance.

Bill and Sandy have another cluster of associations,
which develops around the ideas of failure, decay, and old
age. Bill's absorption with making better movies than Jeff
is an example. Since he obviously does not have the exotic
subjects available to him that Jeff has, his competition is
doomed to failure. In the play, Jeff gets to show his slides
to Bill, but leaves before Bill can show his movies to Jeff.
Bill is also a failure at his job as the letter he describes,
accusing him of "professional inconsistency," indicates. After
the Freeds arrive, Bill tells a story about a fellow employee
named Charlie E. Z., who is obviously a fantasy version of
himself.

The story is that Charlie has started riding up and
down the company elevator naked. Soon he is joined by various other company employees, who surprise people waiting
for the elevator by appearing inside, naked, and then closing
the doors and going to another floor. "The point is that
everybody at Continental Allied loves Charlie E. Z. now.
The letters about 'professional inconsistency' have stopped
coming ... and he's doing just great...." (p. 155) Bill's
fantasy reflects his fear that he is failing at his job.

Sandy's chief association with failure comes at the
end of the play when she tries to explain to Nicky why he
can't have a brother. "The doctor said if you try too hard
the mommy's eggs won't come down right," (p. 183) she
explains in deep humiliation. Later, she says, "When I
looked in the mirror this morning, I saw an old lady who
could only conceive once." (p. 184) Sandy's decay is indicated further by "that bitter salty smell of low tide" (p. 124)
which only she can smell. She repeatedly shakes sand out
of her hair, which suggests to her that her head is "drying
up and leaking" (p. 110) like a worn-out doll's. She believes that her hair is falling out and that she will soon be
"bald as an egg." (p. 111) And she says several times,
"When I looked in the mirror this morning, I saw an old
lady. Not old old, just used up." (p. 110)

The only associations concerning the Apples that do

not involve Nicky and are positive are their childhood memories, briefly recalled while Nicky is out of the room. Each
remembers a special birthday party. Sandy recalls: "My
eighth was the best. I invited the entire class. It was on
a Saturday afternoon and we strung white streamers from one
end of the dining room to the other." (p. 130) Bill remembers his eleventh: "That was the birthday I got my red
bike." (p. 130) They also recall playing kissing and petting
games at these parties, but when they begin kissing, inspired
by the recollection, they are interrupted by Nicky. Their
only happy associations are with a past that is no longer possible for them.

Only a few associations cluster around the Freeds
beyond their stories of primitive children, but those that do
are in contrast to the Apples'. Mia and Jeff arrive late because Mia has been presenting a conference paper. Meanwhile, Sandy and Bill have passed the time making animal
noises with Nicky, a striking contrast in the level of sophistication of Sandy's and Mia's occupations. Visually, there
is a contrast between Mia, described as "a fragile beauty."
(p. 142) and Sandy, self-described as an old woman and
dominated by her "giant four-year-old," a grown man.

The Freeds are invariably more favorably represented
in the many contrasts between them and the Apples. Jeff is
a better photographer than Bill. Mia is more beautiful than
Sandy. The food they describe is exotic, almost inedible,
while the Apples describe common foods. The children they
have known have amazing abilities, while Nicky has just
learned to spell his own name. In fact, however, Nicky does
have at least one remarkable skill himself, his cello playing,
which goes unnoticed by his doting parents, who prefer him
helpless.

The exotic language the Freeds use to describe their
adventures is dropped in one instance, however. This exception is Mia's description of pushing the baby back into the
Whan See woman, an act in which she was forced to participate. She says that it was like stuffing a fifty-pound turkey.

This is a significant moment, a turning point in the
play marked by a shift in the pattern of associations. The
Freeds, to this point, have described the Whan See in exotic,
positive language. But when Mia describes the "fatal flaw"
of the Whan See, she resorts to this homely, American image of stuffing a turkey because the flaw of the Whan See is

also the flaw of American families such as the Apples.   Jeff
makes the comparison explicit:

> You have to remember, these were a highly
> primitive people who took things literally.   When
> a civilized woman has a baby, she too is posses-
> sive, only in more subtle ways.   She's possessive
> of her birth experience and delights in retelling
> it.   She's possessive of her baby and tries to
> keep him helpless for as long as possible.   Well,
> the Stone Age women were just acting out that
> same possessiveness by reinserting the baby into
> its mother's womb.   Through fetal insertion, you
> see, the primitive mother could experience her
> moment of motherhood over and over and over
> again. (p. 167)

The similarity between the Whan See and the Apples is
pointed up further in Mia and Sandy's dialogue:

> SANDY: I feel so tired all the time.
>   MIA: You know what it felt like?   Stuffing a
>   turkey.   Stuffing a fifty-pound turkey with
>   some little ... hamster.
> SANDY: Nicky ... oh, my Nicky ...
>   MIA: And there was this overpowering cinna-
>   mon smell.   And I started laughing.
> SANDY: Nicky is four today.   My son is four
>   years old.
>   MIA: ... and then they all started laughing,
>   with those light, sighing voices.   All the
>   women wrapped their long arms around
>   each other, threw back their heads and
>   laughed.
> SANDY: Oh, Mia!   You should have a baby.   It's
>   so wonderful! (p. 169)

The flaw in the Whan See is the same as the flaw in
the Apples.   Both are overly possessive of their children.
The Apples' lives revolve around Nicky; he is the only point
of contact in their marriage, and the only attraction they
can offer to potential converts such as the Freeds.   Just as
the Whan See try to prolong the moment of birth, the Apples
try to prolong Nicky's helpless infancy.   Sandy is delighted
to pretend with Nicky that he is a baby again, and to retell
the story of his birth.   When he shows an ability beyond his
years by playing the cello, Sandy and Bill ignore him.   They

prefer to think that his greatest achievement is being able
to pull his wagon around the room.

The Whan See and the Apples are associated in the
play as two primitive "tribes" which are overly possessive
of their children. The more sophisticated Freeds visit both
the Whan See and the Apples, and seem to have learned to
avoid the limitations of either life by observing them. Thus,
the clusters of associations reveal a hierarchy, but one based
on family models, with the Whan See and the Apples at the
lower, primitive level, and the glamorous Freeds above them.

Because the hierarchy is not strictly sexual, it does
not fit the definition of feminist drama. Instead, it indicates
a play in which the society oppresses those who choose to
live as a nuclear family, absorbed in a limited life revolving
around their children. The Freeds, although they have higher
status than the Apples, are not oppressors; they simply keep
themselves detached from the society as intellectual onlook-
ers, playing the role of anthropologist in their own culture
as well as in others.

The play reveals the self-chosen limitations of men
as well as of women in the nuclear family. The Apples are
not realistically portrayed; they are a satiric exaggeration
of the typical American family. Like Bill, the play suggests,
the typical American husband and father is competitive and
fearful of failure in the work world, emotionally immature
and self-absorbed. Like Sandy, the American housewife is
pre-occupied with housecleaning, too attentive to her children and yet resentful of them. She is prematurely aged and
unattractive, almost asexual. Nicky represents the worst
qualities of American children. He is precocious and demanding, dominating the lives of his parents, a physical
giant as real children are often emotional giants in their
family relationships.

Nicky is not just spoiled and brattish, but actually
rebellious, alternately exploiting and protesting his parents'
over-attentiveness in the first act. Their attempts to coerce
Nicky into a more submissive role, followed by their efforts
to seduce the Freeds into taking on roles in the nuclear family, make up the play's pattern of symbolic action.

Pattern of Symbolic Action

The pattern of symbolic action in Birth and After Birth

is in two related parts.   In the first act, the Apples try to
coerce Nicky into accepting a submissive, infantile role in
the family.   In the second act, they try to persuade the
Freeds to accept the role of parents in a nuclear family like
the Apples' own.   From the opening moments of the play,
the Apples attempt to control Nicky's behavior to meet their
own expectations.   While he is opening his gifts, Bill encourages him to be childlike for the movie camera: "Atta
boy, Nick, show 'em how good you can play.   Look at Daddy
and play something.   Over this way ... look at Daddy!"
(p. 105)   Nicky does play with his toys, but dashes around
the room too fast for Bill to film him, infuriating his father.

Sandy encourages him to act like a baby, lying in her
arms and gurgling.   Nicky plays for awhile, but when he
discovers the game will not get him what he wants, a glass
of grape juice, he switches from saying, "Baby firsty, baby
still firsty," to a plain "I want grape juice." (p. 117)   The
game that wins Nicky the most attention is fainting.   For
playing this completely passive and infantile game, he wins
his parents' panicky attempts to revive him and their complete forgetfulness of the temper tantrum that immediately
preceded it.   When he wakes up, his parents reward him
with one of the only quiet, affectionate moments in the play.

Whether Nicky has submitted to his parents' attempts
to cast him as the infantile child in the ideal nuclear family
is still an open question at the end of Act I.   In Act II,
however, he expresses his loyalty toward the nuclear family
by participating wholeheartedly in the birth charade for Mia.
By the end of the play, Nicky seems contented as a member
of the family unit, hopeful of increasing it by a baby brother,
and anxious to watch his father's home movies, with or without the Freeds.

There is no doubt, however, that the Apples' struggle
to impose the nuclear family pattern on the Freeds is a failure.   Mia finally responds to their most massive attempt,
the birth charade, by fainting as Nicky did, but in her case
fainting is an escape from their attentions, rather than an
invitation for more.

The Apples' efforts begin as soon as the Freeds arrive, with the conflict most evident between the two women.
Although Sandy sometimes frames her complaint against
both the Freeds: "Neither of them wants children!" (p. 126),
it is Mia who worries her the most: "Imagine being a woman

and not wanting to experience childbirth." (p. 127)   Bill is
less involved in the problem.   "Jeffrey and Mia have been
married for twelve years," he points out.   "I don't think
they're going to change their minds about having children at
Nicky's birthday party." (p. 127)   But when Sandy objects to
this defeatist attitude, he adds, "Just because I understand
their reasons for not wanting children doesn't mean I agree
with them!" (p. 128)   And in the second act, both Bill and
Nicky assist Sandy in imposing the birth charade on Mia.

Sandy's motive for wanting the Freeds to have children is not quite explicit in the play, but it is easy to uncover.
What if the Freeds changed their minds, she speculates, "because of us and Nicky and how happy we all are." (p. 127)
Yet she admits: "Of course, we don't get to travel like they
do, we don't have their kind of freedom," (p. 140) and "of
course, Mia looks younger than me." (p. 141)   In fact, Mia
and Jeff seem to be in a happier situation than Sandy and
Bill in every respect.   Only their childlessness enables
Sandy to pity them and thus to feel superior: "It's just pathetic.   Trying to have her own family through other people's
children, and not even American children, but poor starving--"
(p. 141)   And by the same token, only by Mia becoming a
mother would she lose her career and actually be Sandy's
equal in situation.

Sandy is well aware of the limitations a child would
put on Jeff and Mia.   "For the first few years you'd have to
stay home.   You certainly wouldn't want to bring a newborn
into the Sahara Desert or anything," (p. 170) she says.
"You'd have to forget about your career for six or seven
years, maybe even longer."   In that case, Mia would be like
Sandy, no longer more beautiful, more travelled, and as her
name suggests, "Freed," but a trapped and limited housewife like Sandy.

Mia, however, is horrified by the Whan See custom
of repeated re-births and apparently just as horrified by the
American version of that custom.   She struggles against the
birth charade, screaming, "God! Help me!" (p. 173)   Finally, she resists by passing out and remaining unconscious
until it is time to leave.

The pattern of symbolic action reveals a struggle to
impose, not just the experience of having a child, but the
whole limiting, possessive life of the nuclear family, first

on the youngest member of that family, and then on a child-
less couple who have escaped this life. In Nicky's case, the
Apples seem to be succeeding as the play ends. But the
Freeds go off to study an urban culture at the end of the
play, apparently unaffected by the encounter.

Because the Apples are struggling to convert others
to their limited life, rather than to free themselves, this
play does not fit the definition of feminist drama. Certainly,
Sandy's situation is one with which many women would identify. Her life is an exaggeration of the plight of the housewife, whose confining dependence is the antithesis of the
feminist ideal. Sandy's role is one which many feminists
have identified and rejected in their own lives. Thus, because audience members may recognize themselves in Sandy,
she is not an unsympathetic character despite her attempts
to coerce Jeff and Mia.

Also, her dream of converting the Freeds is so obviously hopeless that it never seems a serious threat. As
Bill says, "They're not interested in having a beautiful baby,
they're interested in primitive children!" (p. 128), and it
does seem unlikely that the Apples' happiness will convert
them, particularly since the Apples fight continually. It is
true, as Bill tells Sandy, that, "You don't give a good shit
if I'm fired! All you care about is playing your moronic
baby games with Nicky!" (p. 117) But this is as much
Sandy's loss as it is Bill's. She seems totally without inter-
ests apart from Nicky, even to her disinterest in Bill's sexual
advances to her, which she resists by saying, "Don't, Nicky
might come in." (p. 132) The only goal to which we see
her aspire is converting Mia to the joys of total motherhood,
a goal that is obviously unrealistic. Thus, Sandy is a pitiful
character, doomed to failure, as is Bill. Mia and Jeff, on
the other hand, are not particularly sympathetic nor even
very thoroughly drawn characters. The result is a rather
sympathetic satire, in which the Apples are treated with compassion.

But because the Apples do not resist their situation,
trying to coerce others into adopting it instead, the play
cannot be considered feminist by the definition employed in
this work. Although the Apples are oppressed by their society, their oppression is based on their family life rather than
their sex. Women can identify with Sandy's plight, but the
play is almost as much about Bill, whose role is only slightly
limiting. Nor do the Apples struggle to achieve autonomy.

Instead, they struggle to convert others to their situation,
first Nicky and then the Freeds.   Because the Apples offer
no resistance to their oppressive environment, scene dominates completely in this play.

Agent:Scene Ratio

It is obvious to the audience that Sandy--depressed,
tired, and balding--is in a pitiable state.   But it is not obvious to Sandy.   Between fits of depression, she wonders
why the Freeds are not converted to the Apples' way of life
by observing their blissful condition.   So thoroughly are she
and Bill dominated by their environment that they do not even
realize their oppression.   Instead, they try to convert the
Freeds, who are obviously happier and in a better situation
than they.

Scene dominates in this play to the extent that the
agents, Sandy and Bill, voluntarily sacrifice themselves to
maintain and spread the unjust order.   Burke would call
this an act of Mortification to preserve the existing hierarchy.
This order is not entirely a sexual hierarchy, since Bill and
Sandy have different roles but are almost equally oppressed.
However, it is an unjust and oppressive system, a fact that
Sandy and Bill ignore, devoting themselves instead to making
converts to it.   If Mia and Jeff could be converted, they
would no longer serve as a reminder to the Apples of another
life outside the system.   Instead, their conversion would
serve to reinforce the Apples' way of life.

Because scene is emphasized, the play is allied to
the materialistic philosophy.   Bill, Sandy, and eventually
Nicky regard themselves as a family, locked in "an endless
embrace"; they are a unit of society rather than three individuals.   Thus the individual spirit is subordinated, as expected in a materialistic play.   The play should also reflect
determinism, and the Apples' lives are completely determined
by their society.   They learn nothing from their encounter
with the Freeds, and nothing in the play suggests that they
will ever change.

Conclusion

Birth and After Birth comments on the protective and
possessive, limiting nuclear family in its portrayal of the

Apple family's attempt to convert the Freeds to their own
way of life. The associational clusters create a contrast between the simple-minded, banal, decaying Apple family absorbed in their domineering child, and the exotic, liberated
Freeds. Like the Whan See, the primitive tribe most repul-
sive to the Freeds, the Apples are figuratively "child-eaters"
who would like to keep Nicky a helpless baby and re-live the
moment of his birth again and again.

The pattern of symbolic action in the play demonstrates
the Apples' attempts, first to keep Nicky in submission, then
to convert the Freeds to their own life style. Both attempts
fail, but although the Freeds escape, the Apples are still
certain that they themselves are "the happiest family in the
world."

Because the play does not depict an agent struggling
for autonomy in an unjust socio-sexual hierarchy, it cannot
be considered a feminist drama by the definitions employed
earlier. While the Apples are oppressed by societal forces,
they do not oppose these forces. Instead, they ignore their
own oppression and attempt to convert the Freeds. Their
unsuccessful struggle is toward the Freeds' conversion, not
toward their own autonomy. The Apples are completely controlled by their environment from the beginning of the play
until the end, reflecting the play's deterministic philosophy.

Because the play deals with characters and a situation
with which women can identify, and because it was written
by a woman and published in an anthology of women's theatre,
it provides an interesting subject for analysis by the methods
employed in this work. The examination of associational clusters and pattern of symbolic action suggested by Burke reveal
that the play's rhetorical motive is not feminist. But they
also reveal what its rhetorical motive is: to satirize the
American nuclear family and its attempt to convert others
to its own, ridiculously limited situation.

The definition of feminism employed here, somewhat
more stringent than the one suggested by Honor Moore and
accepted in popular culture, allows distinctions to be made
among plays of interest to women. This play, because it
represents both Bill and Sandy as oppressed by their society
and because it does not show them struggling against this
oppression, can be distinguished from plays in which the
rhetorical motive is feminist. Thus, this method of analysis
permits the critic to distinguish among somewhat similar

plays those that are feminist in their rhetorical motive. It
also permits the elucidation of the rhetorical motive of plays
that are not feminist, and their comparison with plays that
are.

Notes

1. Honor Moore, ed., The New Women's Theatre (New
    York: Random House, 1977) p. xxxvi.

2. Ibid, p. 101.

3. Ibid, p. xii.

4. Ibid, p. 101.

5. Ibid.

6. Ibid.

7. Tina Howe, Birth and After Birth in The New Women's
    Theatre, p. 104. Subsequent page references to this
    play in this chapter will be given in the text following
    the quote.

Chapter 6

PLAYS BY FEMINIST THEATRE GROUPS

Introduction

      The feminist impulse in drama is by no means limited
to the past few years of political feminist activity in the
United States. Nor has all feminist drama been written by
those politically involved in feminism, as past chapters of
this study should indicate. However, the recent past has
seen the growth of a new and politically related expression
of feminism: the feminist theatre group. Any study devoted
to feminist drama, as this one is, should include an examination of the work of such groups.

      In organization and in the style of drama that femi-
nist theatre groups perform, they draw heavily on the prece-
dent of communal theatres of the sixties. However, the
rhetorical strategies they employ are uniquely adapted to
group expression of the feminist impulse. Because these
scripts are written explicitly as feminist rhetoric, their
strategies are also more direct and obvious than those in
the scripts written by individuals.

      As a result, these plays are often less complex in
their development, and less analysis is required to compre-
hend their rhetorical intent. This chapter departs from
those preceding it in providing many examples of the drama
of feminist theatre groups, rather than analyzing one play
at length. Four characteristic rhetorical strategies emerge
from the study of the plays; however, these strategies have
not evolved in any historical order that can be generalized
from group to group. Each strategy will be described and
illustrated with several plays as examples. One play employing each strategy will then be briefly analyzed using the
method and definitions advocated in this study.

      This organization permits an overview of the rhetorical
strategies employed by feminist theatre groups. Analysis of
the scripts points up some of their limitations, as well as
limitations of this method in dealing with experimental theat-

rical forms. The fresh and direct approach taken in the
scripts suggests some future directions that feminist drama
may take. Adaptations in the method employed here may be
necessary if it is to continue to be relevant to the study of
feminist drama.

Feminist Theatre Groups

        Since 1969 when Anselma dell' Olio directed the first
production of the New Feminist Repertory in New York,
groups dedicated to expressing feminism in dramatic art
have multiplied. A November 1977 issue of Theatre News
listed seventy-three feminist theatre groups known to be active across the United States. [1]

        The generalizations presented here are based on the
study of interviews, scripts, and printed materials from five
feminist theatre groups in different parts of the country.
The groups are: The Westbeth Playwrights Feminist Collective in New York City; the B & O Theatre, which originated
in Champaign, Illinois; The Rhode Island Feminist Theatre
(RIFT) in Providence; Circle of the Witch in Minneapolis;
and the Boulder Feminist Theatre in Colorado. [2] The earliest of these groups began in 1971, and all but Westbeth are
still in existence, although sometimes in altered form.

        All of the groups except Boulder are communally
organized, following the custom of radical theatres of the sixties. The communal organization also expresses their rejection of the hierarchical organization of traditional theatres,
which they identify with patriarchal values. Westbeth, because it was specifically a playwrights' collective, hired professional actors, and group members did not perform. The
other groups hold open auditions to find actors as they are
needed. These groups regard all of their members as actors. RIFT considers its male actors to be full-fledged
members of the group; the others simply find male volunteers
to act when required by the script.

        All of the groups play to a variety of audiences, femi-
nist as well as general ones. Some of these audiences pay
to attend, but all of the groups run on a day-to-day financial
basis, using grant money as well as gate receipts to cover
expenses. None of the groups pay their members regular
salaries.

        Expression of the feminist consciousness of the mem-

bers and education of audiences in feminist ideas are goals
shared by all of the groups. All have explored a variety of
presentational styles and rhetorical devices in meeting this
goal. Devices common to more than one group's experimen-
tation include: 1) the sex-role reversal device; 2) the presentation of historical figures as role models; 3) satire of
traditional sex roles; 4) the direct portrayal of women in
oppressive situations.

The Sex-Role Reversal

        Disguising a character in the clothing of the opposite
sex is, of course, a device as old as comedy. In recent
years, playwrights have used whiteface to rhetorical effect
in reversing the roles of the races. However, the use of
sex-role reversal as a rhetorical device is unique to feminist drama.

        Men and women are shown playing the reverse of
their usual sex roles in this device, with the result that
the existence of sex-role differences and the unjust status of
women becomes humorously apparent. The skits and plays
based on this device vary in whether they provide realistic
explanations for the reversal of roles, in how humorously
they treat this situation, and in whether they focus on a particular injustice or attempt to show the universality of sex
discrimination.

        Two skits from the Westbeth collective employing
this device are "Restaurant Blackout" by Patricia Horan,
and "The Pick Up Schtick" by Dolores Walker and A. Piotrowski. [3] In "Restaurant Blackout," a man and a woman
enter a restaurant, order drinks and leave, but the woman
seizes every opportunity to make the chivalric, "male" gesture: calling the waiter, lighting her date's cigarette, and
paying for the drinks. When he says he feels "rented," the
woman responds, "Oh, baby, that's a terrible hang-up to
have. What do you say we go to my place for a nightcap
and talk it over?" In "The Pick Up Schtick," a woman introduces herself to a man in the company cafeteria. She explains that she is in personnel: "Salaries. Promotions. I
decide all of that. And you're a very promising young man."
She proceeds to make a date with him in an aggressive manner, and ends by telling him to wear a particular pair of
slacks she has seen him in, "dark blue, a bit tight."

These two skits employ the device within a fairly realistic framework. In both cases it would be possible for a
woman, simply by so choosing, to behave in this way to a
man. Because the skits focus on courting behavior, traditionally a theme of comedy, both can be broadly humorous
in style. The men's astonishment and distaste at their treatment make the message obvious: men would not like to be
condescended to as they condescend to women. "The Pick
Up Schtick," by showing that the woman, because she heads
personnel, has economic power over the man, suggests a
more serious reason why women might submit to such con-
descension, just as the man does in the skit.

"Family, Family," a short play by Sally Ordway of
the Westbeth collective, shows the limited sex role a little
girl learns while growing up in the nuclear family.[4] However, the father, son, and boyfriends are played by women,
the mother and daughter by men. The story breaks down
when the man playing the daughter suddenly objects to his
lines. The other man agrees that their lines are foolish
and that families "aren't like this,"[5] but the women in the
cast defend the play and offer to tell what happened to the
protagonist in later life. "Margaret got away from her family. She made something of herself. Eventually, she became quite a well-known shrink specializing in the psyches
of women. She never married, but had several interesting
lovers, men and women." The man who played Margaret
says, "That's not what happened at all!"[6] and leaves, followed by the man who had played the mother. After a blackout, new cast members, representing another nuclear family,
begin the play again.

Here again, the revelation of the "play-within-a-play"
at the end places the reversal of sex roles within a realistic
framework. It also enables the skit to make two related
points. First, in the "play-within-a-play," the subtle, social
oppression usually experienced by women becomes obvious
when experienced by men. The parents treat their two children very differently, encouraging achievement and competitiveness in the son (played by a woman) and passivity and
physical attractiveness in the daughter (played by a man.)
When the "play-within-a-play" breaks down, a second point
is made. The men object that it is not realistic, but since
it is a string of the most familiar clichés, it is unlikely that
this is their real objection. The "mother's" first line out of
character--"I hate saying my lines!"--touches on a more
likely motive.[7] The men in the play simply feel humiliated

saying the things that women say, and being treated as women
are treated.   The humiliation of playing a woman's role is
thus illustrated.   Because the "play-within-a-play" telescopes
the whole process of growing up, it makes a broad, universal
statement on discrimination.   The telescoping also creates an
episodic, broadly painted series of scenes which lends itself
to farcical humor and slapstick.

A short play by Myrna Lamb, developed by the New
Feminist Repertory Theatre in New York, should also be
mentioned here, although not created by one of the five groups
studied.   The play, entitled, "But What Have You Done for
Me Lately?", was first performed at the Redstocking abortion hearings. [8]   It shows a man who has been artificially
impregnated by a fellow scientist, a woman he had impregnated during a love affair when they were students together.
All his arguments for ending his pregnancy are shown to be
similar to women's arguments favoring legalized abortion.
Finally, a "jury"--sometimes taken from the audience--de-
cides whether he deserves an abortion.   In the published
ending, he is judged by a panel of women who have experienced personal tragedies because abortion was unavailable
to them.   They grant him the abortion because they do not
judge him fit to be a parent.

In this play there is no attempt at realism in explaining the sex-role reversal, nor is the style humorous.   Rather,
a somber mood is set by the woman's description of her own
childbearing:

> I suffered a labor complicated by an insufficient
> pelvic span and a lack of dilation.   I spent three
> days in company with other women who were car-
> ried in and out of the labor room screaming curses
> and for their mothers....   Finally there was a
> last-ditch high forceps, a great tearing mess, and
> the emergence of a creature that I fully expected
> to see turned purple with my own terrible hatred
> and ripped to shreds by the trial of its birth. [9]

A bitter, ironic humor is apparent, however, in the woman's
responses to the man's protests against his pregnancy.   When
he says that the fetus's life is not as important as his own,
she responds:

> Yes, I understand how you feel.   But how would
> it be if every pregnancy brought about in error or

> ignorance or through some evil or malicious or
> even well-meaning design were terminated because
> of the reluctance or the repugnance of the host?
> Surely the population of the world would be so
> effectively decimated as to render wholly redundant
> the mechanisms of lebensraum, of national politics,
> of hunger as a method, of greed as a motive, of
> war itself as a method. [10]

In keeping with its limited and highly serious topic, abortion,
this play is the least humorous of those examined despite the
non-realistic premise on which it is based.

  The longest and most subtly developed example of
this device among the plays examined is RIFT's full-length
play, The Johnnie Show. [11] The action in this play moves
back and forth between segments of a talk show similar to
the "Tonight" show with Johnny Carson, and episodes from
the life of Mark, one of Johnnie's guests, a few days before
his appearance on the show. In the last scene, the two
threads of the plot meet when Mark appears as Johnnie's
last guest. In this play men do not have women's names,
nor are they supposedly able to bear children. But the inter-
action between men and women in Mark's family and on television gradually reveals a world in which women dominate
in every sphere of activity and men are valued primarily as
sex objects.

  The play opens with Edie McMann, Johnnie's co-
hostess, "warming up" the audience with a few jokes, and
announcing that tonight will be "Boys' Night" on the show.
Then Johnnie, a woman, enters with a typical Johnny Carson
monologue on Watergate, streaking, and Edie's drinking hab-
its, plus the one about "the recent rash of obscene phone
calls that have been plaguing gentlemen in the city."[12] A
commercial for "Singl-Boy Creme Rinse" follows the monologue, after which the scene shifts to Mark's house, where
his family has prepared a surprise birthday party for him.

  In the course of the first home scene, the audience
learns that Mark recently won the Mr. California contest, a
contest he entered hoping to "expose the sexism of the beauty
industry and show how it is symbolic of the oppression of
all males in this country."[13] Mark considers himself a
member of the Maleist movement--or Boys' Lib, as his disapproving family calls it. The birthday party breaks up
early when Mark's mother must leave for a business meeting,
disappointing his father, who has prepared an elaborate meal.

In succeeding scenes, the Johnnie Show introduces other guests. Fred Walker, a champion in the walking event of the Gentlemen's Olympics, says he will probably retire after the next Olympics and raise a family. Caesar Schlamonz, an aging movie star, is recalled as the "dumb blonde" in old detective films. Dr. June Elliott, an expert in male sexuality, explains the "deep-rooted, you might say, instinctive or primal fears regarding sexual intercourse" found in almost every "boy or gentleman."[14]

In alternating scenes Mark's father tries to put the romance back in his marriage, but his wife, preoccupied with business, rejects his attempts. Mark tries to intervene on the side of his father, but angers both parents, who are also afraid that Mark's appearance on the Johnnie Show will embarrass the family. The last scene is on the Johnnie Show, where the final guest, Mark, is introduced. Mark attempts to air his views on the Maleist movement, but is continually led off the track, made fun of and obliquely criticized by Johnnie and her guests. The play closes at the end of the program.

The method of analysis employed in previous chapters of this study can, of course, be applied to a play like The Johnnie Show, which is based on the sex-role reversal. The clusters of associations define a socio-sexual hierarchy in this play, and the pattern of symbolic action reveals an agent struggling for autonomy. But women are the "mounters" in this hierarchy, and the agent struggling for autonomy is a man.

Most of the associations in The Johnnie Show are forms of address or descriptions of one character by another. Mary K addresses her sons as "baby son" and "gorgeous," and calls her husband "Dennie" rather than "Dennis." Dennis calls his wife by her full name, and urges Mark to spend more time on his appearance because "you've got good looks and an attractive figure, you're extremely fortunate, and it's a shame to let it all go to waste by not taking care of your appearance the way you should."[15] Fred, Mark's brother, calls him "Beautiful." Mark on the other hand, says Lou Ann, Fred's girlfriend, treats Fred like "a wind-up toy." Fred also asks for less rough language at the dinner table to avoid offending "Dad's little pink ears." Within this family, the associations create a hierarchy in which men are toys, babies, or gorgeous bodies, not the seriously treated, fully human beings that women are.

Similarly, on the Johnnie Show, Johnnie and Edie are seldom described or named by anyone. But among the male guests, Caesar Schlamonz is described as a "dumb blonde," a former "pin-up," and "a wonderful father." He is remembered for his role as "the boyfriend of Bonnie Parker in 'Woman on the Run.'" Fred Walker is described by Johnnie as a "stunning body." Johnnie introduces Mark as "a very beautiful and very intelligent young gentleman from Oakland." Only the female doctor is introduced as "a respected professional in her field of urology" without reference to her appearance. In these scenes, too, women are "subjects"; men are "objects," judged primarily on their physical appearance and secondarily on their ability to play subordinate roles, in films and in family life. The clusters form a sexual hierarchy, but it is a hierarchy in which "mounter" and "mounted" are reversed.

The pattern of symbolic action shows Mark struggling for autonomy for himself and his sex against his family's disapproval of Maleism, his brother's submissiveness to Lou Ann, his mother's insensitivity to his father, and everyone's hostility toward his projected appearance on the Johnnie Show. Although he does appear on the show, his planned defense of Maleism fails. Johnnie and the other guests do not permit Mark to complete a sentence without a joke or a double-entendre. Finally, Johnnie brings up the question of how Mark's family feels about his politics, leaving Mark helpless to continue, defeated by society in the form of the media and of his own family. Once again, the play shows an agent struggling for autonomy in an unjust socio-sexual hierarchy, but the agent is male; the "mounters" in the hierarchy are female.

Since the environment, the socio-sexual hierarchy, defeats the agent, the play is deterministic in its philosophy. Although Mark is intelligent, attractive, and articulate, he is doomed to failure. It is impossible for him to assert his autonomy or even protest his situation effectively in a society that treats men as ours treats women. Since his society is a reversed image of ours, the play suggests that men would fare no better than women do in a socio-sexual hierarchy which subordinates them as a sex.

The Johnnie Show serves as an example of the extended use of the sex-role reversal device, a highly artificial and original rhetorical strategy employed by feminist theatre groups. A simpler strategy, and a somewhat later one

in the history of the groups studied, is the creation of role
models by depicting historical characters and events.

Historical Role Models

        Of the five groups studied here, all but one, the
Boulder theatre, has created a historical presentation of
some kind. Circle of the Witch has produced "Time Is Passing: A Story of Minnesota Women at the Turn of the Century."[16] The B & O incorporated an account by a nineteenth-
century Illinois woman, Mrs. Elizabeth Packard, into one of
their productions, "30."[17] The Westbeth collective's last
work was entitled "Jumpin' Salty," and was a bicentennial
show celebrating famous Greenwich Village women.[18] The
RIFT play, "Anne Hutchinson: Rhode Island's First Independent Woman," is the only full-length play on a single historical character in the groups studied.[19]

        "Time Is Passing" and the B & O production resemble
Readers Theatre more than they do conventional plays. Both
draw upon historical documents and are organized around a
theme, rather than around a single protagonist following a
continuous line of action. "Time Is Passing" contains material from journals, letters, speeches, and interviews of
Minnesota women at the turn of the twentieth century, including accounts from Minnesota Indian women, mine workers'
wives, and union organizers. Although many stories are
told, the central theme uniting them is the women's struggle
to overcome their difficult circumstances. The phrase,
"Time Is Passing," is drawn from a letter written by Anna
Rudinitsky to the Women's Trade Union League in 1912:

                Time is passing and everything is missed. I am
                not living. I am just working.... I have been
                thinking. First we must get a living wage and
                then we must get a shorter work day, and many,
                many more girls must do some thinking. It isn't
                that they do not want to think, but they are too
                tired to think and that is the best thing in the
                Union, it makes us think.[20]

The production depicts women struggling against difficult circumstances, caused not only by their sex, but by their pov-
erty, nationality, and lack of education. They prevail against
such circumstances, and are therefore to be admired and
emulated.

The B & O production, which employed not only historical documents but poetry, scenes from plays, and original material, was also organized around a theme: women's madness. The Illinois woman's story from the nineteenth century told of her unjust commitment to an insane asylum by her husband, a minister with whose religious views she differed. She eventually gained her freedom from the asylum, and went on to persuade the Illinois legislature to enact reforms in state insane asylums. Like the women in "Time Is Passing," she struggled for autonomy against circumstances that were worsened, although not wholly caused, by her sexual status.

The Westbeth group's historical production was "Jumpin' Salty," a celebration of famous Greenwich Village women. The program, presented in April of 1975, opened with a "feminist song" sung by Eve Merriam in the courtyard of the Greenwich Village Westbeth housing collective, where the Westbeth playwrights all lived. Performers and musicians then marched through the Village, performing short plays at historical sites associated with the women depicted. Among those represented were Lena Horne, Margaret Sanger, Harriet Tubman, Mable Dodge, and Bessie Hillman. The events depicted ranged from the 1910 Triangle shirtwaist factory fire to an imaginary meeting between Harriet Tubman and Angela Davis on the Underground Railroad.

The play which was presented in Cooper Square, "The Laundry Workers Present Hatpin Bessie," is representative of the style and content of the "Jumpin' Salty" plays. [21] "Hatpin Bessie" is set in 1938, at a union meeting hall in Greenwich Village. The opening scene is a frame play of a Laundry Workers' union meeting at which a tribute to Bessie Hillman is to be presented. The tribute is a show about her life, in which Bessie will play herself. The play-within-a-play, narrated by the chairwoman of the entertainment committee, shows Bessie's life in a highly presentational, humorous style. It opens with a Russian folk dance representing Bessie's Russian-Yiddish background. To avoid the marriage broker, Bessie immigrates to America. On Ellis Island, careless customs officials change her name from "Bashe" to "Bessie." The cast then improvises a train headed for Chicago, where Bessie is seen sewing trousers in a sweatshop. When the foreman announces that he is lowering the piece rate, Bessie leads a walkout. She goes to the president of U. G. W., who laughs at the idea of organizing the tailors, since they are "craftsmen." So, Bessie and her friends or-

ganize a tailors' strike of 30,000 workers on their own. Then
Bessie falls in love and marries another strike leader, Sid-
ney Hillman. Finally, a scene in Smedley's Laundry in New
York shows Bessie's work in organizing the laundry workers.
The play includes two union songs of the period. One, en-
titled "Strike While the Iron Is Hot," closes the play.

Like the plays by the other groups, "Jumpin' Salty"
focuses on local history. Women are depicted overcoming
adverse situations, and asserting their autonomy and their
solidarity with other women in simple and direct style. The
same elements characterize "Anne Hutchinson: Rhode Island's
First Independent Woman," written by RIFT and adapted to
video by Brandon French and Ada McAllister.

The RIFT play begins on the ship carrying the Hutchinson family to America. The Spirit inspires Anne to prophesy when the ship will reach land, antagonizing the ministers
on board. When she arrives, Anne starts a meeting for
women, which is extremely popular and leads to another for
men and women. She also raises an herb garden with which
she doctors the community and assists the old midwife,
Goody Hawkins. All of this further threatens the authority
of the ministers, who spy on her and try to catch her in
errors.

Anne has immigrated to America to be taught by
Brother Cotton, who at first encourages her meetings, but
finally deserts her when she is imprisoned for heresy. Her
women friends, Mary Dyer and Goody Hawkins, remain loyal
and eventually relocate with Anne and her family to another
part of the country when she is banished from the community.
The play ends hopefully, with Anne's vision of a new, demo-
cratic society in which spiritual freedom will be possible.

Although "Anne Hutchinson" presents real, historical
events, it does so in a style that is only partly realistic,
including puppets representing the hostile ministers and a
"Spirit," played by a woman, who appears to Anne to inspire
her and strengthen her faith. When Brother Cotton betrays
Anne, he becomes a puppet like the rest of the ministers.

Like the other historical plays, "Anne Hutchinson"
shows a woman's struggle for autonomy, this time on a
spiritual level. It also emphasizes the elements of Anne
Hutchinson's life that identify her with feminism. This is
accomplished by showing the loyalty of her women followers

and the opposition of the male ministers to a woman's spiritual leadership, as well as by casting a woman as the Spirit. Anne is also shown to have a special concern for the women in the community. When Mary Dyer's deformed child is born, we hear Anne's thoughts:

> I have had fifteen children. I lost two. I also asked why. I also cried, "I don't understand!" Half our women cannot go to meetings because of their duties. And when they do go, what do they understand? What do they hear? We are living by the same puny rules we knew in England, while our women go mad, and our children sicken and die. Women need women. 22

Thus, the feminist aspects of Anne's life are emphasized.

"Anne Hutchinson" is a feminist drama by the definitions employed in this work. The clusters of associations depict a socio-sexual hierarchy, the patriarchal religious state dominating Puritan society. The pattern of symbolic action shows Anne's struggle for spiritual freedom against this hostile hierarchy.

The cluster of associations surrounding the hostile patriarchy is dominated by images of artificiality. Most obvious is the visual image of the grotesque puppets representing the ministers. When these ministers accuse Anne in court, they have numbered her errors, and their speech gradually merges into a mechanical recitation: "Error #20, Error #21, Error #22...."23 Their artificiality is also revealed in their condemnation of the natural. One minister preaches that "we are here to seek salvation (pause), but we are helpless to do anything but evil. For man is (pause) and remains (pause) a brute beast."24 Throughout the play, the ministers relate nature to sexuality and condemn both.

In opposition to this cluster is the one associating Anne with the natural healing of her herb garden. Brother Cotton greets her in her garden singing the Song of Solomon: "I am come into my garden, my sister, my spouse. I have gathered my myrrh with my spice."25 Anne says that these, among the most sensual verses of the Bible, are her favorite. Anne's husband, who is portrayed as completely supportive of her, recalls that he proposed marriage to her in her garden in England: "Oh, how I loved Anne that day. I wanted to lie down in her bed of flowers with her."26 Anne's

herbs are also a source of healing and comfort, especially
to her women friends suffering in frequent childbirth. Mary
Dyer is shown at prayer, trying to resolve her natural sexual desires, her fear of bearing more children, and the
church's preaching against women's licentiousness. Her only
comfort in this conflict is Anne, who brings herbs to ease
her childbearing, and who preaches that "as the woman is
of the man, even so is the man also by the woman, and all
things of God, " refuting the ministers' condemnation of women.
The ministers, however, are suspicious of midwifery and
herb healing, associating it with witchcraft.

Thus, the hierarchy in the play is dominated by the
male power structure in which Church and State support a
highly artificial, unnatural creed. The "mounted" in the
hierarchy are the women, whose natural sexuality is condemned by Church and State. Anne's struggles to oppose
this structure form the pattern of symbolic action.

Throughout the play, Anne insists that she is only
following the guidance of the Spirit in her opposition to the
patriarchy. But since the Spirit is represented by a woman,
this disclaimer does not greatly weaken the impact of her
opposition as a feminist struggle. From the first scene,
when she upstages the ministers' prayer meeting on board
ship with her prophecy, Anne becomes more and more asser-
tive in opposing the patriarchy. At first, her actions are
in support of Brother Cotton against the other ministers, or
are undertaken with Brother Cotton's approval. At her meetings, she criticizes the ministers who speak only of sin, contrasting them with Brother Cotton. And when Mary Dyer's
baby is born deformed, she persuades Brother Cotton to
support their concealment of the deformity, which would open
Mary to suspicions of witchcraft.

After Anne begins holding her own meetings, however,
she abandons Brother Cotton's counsel and acts entirely on
her own initiative. She begins the mixed meetings in her
home without asking his approval, and she defies both the
ministers and the State by giving water to a man being punished in the stocks.

The other women in the community are influenced by
Anne's teaching to assert their autonomy as well. Mary
Dyer refuses to change her dress for a more somber color
at the command of the ministers, causing her husband to
ask if her women's meetings are leading her astray. By the

time Anne comes to trial, she is openly defying the ministers,
supported by her women friends as well as by her husband.
At the end of the play, the pattern of action is resolved in
a more complete transcendence of the unjust hierarchy than
in any of the plays examined so far in this study.   Anne,
banished from the patriarchal society, leaves in triumph to
found a new community.   She is the only character examined
so far who literally founds a new and just order, who achieves
not only personal transcendence but a transformation of her
society.   Thus, this play fits the previously determined definition of feminist drama quite closely, although with two
differences from the plays examined in earlier chapters.

   "Anne Hutchinson," because it is based on historical
fact, must find justifications for viewing Anne as a feminist
without distorting her actual biography, a problem that does
not arise with fictional protagonists.   The historical setting
also lessens the impact of the play's triumphant ending, since
the audience may know that a perfect spiritual society was
not, in fact, achieved.   Secondly, "Anne Hutchinson" is characteristic of plays written by groups in emphasizing the inter-
dependence of women almost as much as the individual's autonomy.   At the end of the play, Anne says that she has been
wrong to preach at meetings.   In the new community, "we
shall all speak at meetings; rejoice and be exceedingly glad."[27]

   Anne's triumph at the end of the play makes it an
idealistic drama in which the agent transcends the oppressive
scene.   Such idealism is typical of plays that offer historical
figures as role models.   Their optimistic conclusions are
designed to encourage imitation of the positive role models
by audience members.   A device that centers on negative
role models instead is the satire of traditional feminine
stereotypes.

Satirizing Sexual Stereotypes

   All five of the groups studied have satirized sexual
stereotypes of women in one or more of their productions.
Sometimes this type of satire was a part of their earliest
performances, and was later replaced by more serious forms
showing positive images of women, such as the historical
plays in the last section.   In other groups, such satire has
been a recurrent device that is still employed in productions.
Two groups, the B & O and RIFT, have improvised satirical
characters without writing scripts for them.   The other three

groups have all performed review-style productions which include material satirizing women's stereotypical roles.

The characters developed by Judy Sarver of the B & O
and by members of RIFT are difficult to discuss without
written scripts as support. However, interviews with the
actors, attendance at performances of these characters, and
newspaper accounts permit some generalizations about this
style of drama. With no knowledge of each other's work,
these two groups have developed characters that show surprising similarities in the method by which they were created,
and in their rhetorical strategies.

The RIFT Clowns of the Stars and Moon developed
from workshops in the Le Coq method of clowning. In this
method, the actors begin by choosing costume pieces, and
then gradually develop a walk and a voice to suit the costume.
Thus, the clown character is allowed to form almost spontaneously from the subconscious mind of the actor. Similarly,
Judy Sarver of the B & O began her characters by visiting
a friend who saved old clothes. The clothes she tried on
inspired several characters, whose costumes she later added
to by visiting the Salvation Army and by borrowing from her
family. Eventually Sarver dropped some of these characters,
but those she still performs continue to develop, gaining new
lines at almost every performance. Thus, in both cases,
the clowns or characters were inspired by costumes, instead
of gaining costumes after their development. In both cases,
the characters arose spontaneously from the actor's mind,
and continue to change and develop during performances.

Usually these characters are a stereotypical image of
traditional woman: doting mother; aggressive but ladylike
clubwoman; seductress. However, both Sarver's characters
and the RIFT clowns differ from traditional satire in the
degree of sympathy with which they are presented. Audiences
are expected to laugh at them, but also to feel a twinge of
recognition of a character like the one performed by Pam-
ela Carchio of RIFT, named "I'm Your Mother and I'm So
Proud and Happy."

One of Sarver's characters, originally inspired by a
maternity dress, is named "The Pregnant Woman." "The
Pregnant Woman's story began to evolve," Sarver recalls,
"and I realized as the story came out, that what I had here
was not just comedy. What I had here was pathos, too....
I didn't have to be funny. I would be as real as possible.

And that was funny enough.   And yet, that's sad enough, too."[28]

Ada McAllister of RIFT says that the characters are always partly autobiographical, which may account for the sympathy with them that actors and audiences feel.   Terry Kennedy, reviewing the RIFT clowns, promised audiences:

> You will recognize your faults and smile at their universality.   More than likely you will also worry that the lights will come on too quickly, before you have time for all that water in your eyes to dry up.   Believe me, these clowns will tell you things about yourself that you thought only your pillow knew.[29]

The characters, then, evoke a compassionate kind of satiric response, in which the audience is asked not only to laugh at the traditional roles these characters play, but to recognize that they have also played such roles, and to forgive themselves.

A more conventional satire of sex roles is found in the musical reviews some groups have presented, such as Boulder's "The Boyfriend,"[30] Westbeth's "?!,"[31] and "Sexpot Follies" by Circle of the Witch.[32]   These productions include skits with "gag" punchlines, singing, and dancing. In satirizing traditional roles, they also show an unusual compassion for the characters satirized, and often reveal the rebelliousness under their submissive surfaces.

A poem by Susan Yankowitz, performed as part of Westbeth's "?!," is entitled "The Chicken." The persona, who is both a barnyard chick and the "chick" which is slang for "woman," begins by predicting a violent end for herself:

> I was born for it,
> a natural blonde
> so smooth and golden
> that men drool.
> Oh yes I know that I
> look good enough to eat.
> But I was not given breasts
> so you could chew on them
> or bones for you to suck.

The chick is afraid to rebel openly, so instead she plays the role expected of her:

> There's no way out of it.
> Cooped up here with wings
> that do not fly, I flap
> and flutter, I cuddle
> and peep: Sweet little,
> helpless little, darling
> little me. Oh, don't you
> love me? Oh won't you spare
> this soft sweet chick?[33]

Her acceptance of a traditional role is a strategy for survival. By recognizing this, the poem shifts the blame from
the actor of the role to the threatening society that forces
this strategy.

"Sexpot Follies" also blames societal forces for the
stereotypical roles women play, making it clear that the
women are not to blame. It adds to this impression by
showing the women starting to rebel against their roles as
the review progresses. "Sexpot Follies" opens with singing
and tap dancing to a parody of "I'm a Little Teapot":

> I'm a little sexpot, short and sweet
> Look at my body, ain't I neat?
> When you ball me over, then I shout
> Sock it to me, baby, let it all hang out.[34]

Verses of this song continue throughout the review, and are
interspersed with monologues and scenes played by actresses
from the chorus line, introduced by a female M. C.

These scenes show a variety of stereotypical roles,
such as "teenyboppers" wishing they could be as thin as
magazine models in order to attract boys. In another scene,
one woman recommends a vaginal deodorant to another in a
parody of television commercials. A third scene shows
"hippie-chicks" discussing the same diet and boy problems
that the teenagers did. But at the end of this scene, one of
them begins to rebel: "I went to another meeting last night
and it happened again. I ended up making coffee and typing
envelopes, while the men made the heavy decisions. Well,
damn it, I had something to say!"[35] Finally, the chorus
line is shown after a rehearsal, planning a strike because
one member has been fired.

The chorus girls gradually begin leaving the line,
until the M. C. is left alone on stage. At this point, rapists

in coats, masks, and hoods advance on the M. C. while
statistics on the frequency of rape are recited. After the
last statistic, the M. C. screams, and there is a blackout.
After the blackout, the rapists come forward, remove their
hoods, and explain that they represent institutions "raping"
women in subtle ways. Government, mass media, education,
the nuclear family, and institutionalized religion are represented.

        Then, the same actors describe an alternate govern-
ment, media, education, and family. The play ends with a
song, "Hang in There":

            We have learned so much about living
            Since we've had to stay alive
            We used to think, well hell it ain't worth it
            But now, united we will survive.[36]

The rhetorical message in "Sexpot Follies" is so obviously
stated that analysis by the definitions employed in this work
becomes almost unnecessary. The socio-sexual hierarchy
is named and condemned directly in the final scene. Earlier
associations clustering around this patriarchy relate mostly
to the mass media, rather than to all the institutions named
at the end.

        For example, the teenyboppers idolize models in
Seventeen magazine. The hippie-chicks read a Clairol ad
and discuss bleaching their hair. One monologue consists
almost entirely of a list of beauty products:

            So I washed my hair with Breck shampoo, followed
            by a Clairol hair rinse and a Toni home permanent,
            then brushed with ultrabrite [the rest of the prod-
            ucts named are not capitalized in the script], put
            on my ice-blue secret anti-perspirant, my femi-
            nique hygiene spray, cover girl sheer foundation,
            yardley natural eyeshadow, max factor eyeliner,
            maybelline lovely eyes mascara, revlon blush-on,
            love's fresh lemon cologne, legs look alive panty-
            hose, playtex living bra, dayton's country girl
            dress and I had lots of boyfriends, but they were
            BORING ... and so was I.[37]

The socio-sexual hierarchy, then, is associated with the
mass media selling an artificial ideal of beauty, an objectification of women with a capitalistic motive.

Opposing this hierarchy, the pattern of symbolic action shows the actresses, as various characters and as chorus girls, gradually realizing their oppression and beginning to rebel against it. This rebellion culminates in the chorus girls' walkout. Up to this point, it would be easy to see the women's oppression as their own choice. Although the influence of mass media is depicted pervading the lives of characters in the skits, the women can and do simply reject this false ideal of beauty. The final scene, which breaks the pattern of the play, emphatically shifts responsibility from the women to the hierarchy itself. Unfortunately, its very obviousness breaks with the witty, review style of the rest of the play, abandons satire, and ends the play on a surprisingly verbose and solemn note.

"Sexpot Follies," like most productions by feminist theatre groups, portrays many women's experiences and finds a solution in women's solidarity rather than following one individual's solitary struggle for autonomy. However, the struggle for women's autonomy against an unjust socio-sexual hierarchy can be traced in the progression of brief scenes that comprise the play. Like the other presentations that satirize traditional sexual roles, this play portrays the actors of such roles sympathetically, blaming their adoption of these roles on the oppressive society. As a rhetorical strategy, such satire emphasizes the negative, but does so humorously and without condemning those who are satirized.

Portrayal of Women's Oppression

The most direct rhetorical device employed by feminist theatre groups is the portrayal of women oppressed by their society. This strategy wins sympathy simply by showing the injustice of women's treatment. However, because this strategy does not show even unsuccessful attempts at transcending oppression, it is in some ways the least positive of the devices examined.

A brief and effective example of this device is Dolores Walker's "Abide in Darkness," originally performed as part of Westbeth's Rape-In in 1971. [38] The play has only two characters, Esther and Ellen, who live in the same large apartment building in New York. Ellen, whose hobby is meeting new people, drops in on Esther. Esther nervously admits her after unlocking four bolts. She explains that she has been very careful since "it happened," but never says

what "it" was.   Now she does not use her mailbox and has
no phone.   As she talks, Esther constantly adds jackets,
shawls, and gloves to her costume.   She tries futilely to de-
tain Ellen, who is disconcerted by Esther's manner.   Finally,
Ellen leaves.   Esther locks the door, pulls back the curtains,
leaves one light on, and strips down to her slip.   Footsteps
are heard on the fire escape.   Esther says:

> It is my imagination.   It is always my imagination.
> The trains are not running, the power is off, the
> mail has stopped, I can not breathe.   It is my
> imagination.   Nothing is happening, nothing at all.[39]

Her window is heard breaking as the play ends.

This play has a sense of movement and progress to
it, because the audience gradually gathers the impression
that Esther is paranoid, and then realizes at the last moment
that her behavior may be bizarre, but her fear is an appropriate response to her situation.   In fact, however, the play
represents a static situation.   Esther's life of fear is a con-
stant; only the audience's understanding of it progresses.

The static quality of the oppressive situation in "Abide
in Darkness" is typical of plays employing this device.   Less
typical is the play's slightly "fantastic" style.   That is, while
the play makes a realistic point about women's fears, the
audience is likely to discount Esther's recurrent rape as not
literally true to life.

Most plays employing this device represent the oppressive situation more realistically.   "Lady in the Corner"
by Circle of the Witch employs both realistic and non-realistic
styles, opening with a mime that represents a "collective
woman's life."[40]   The mime begins with a sleeping, pregnant
woman, who gives birth.   A second woman represents her
child growing from infancy to adolescence.   A third is the
teenager who mimes giving the rock she has been kicking to
a fourth actor, representing the adult woman.   The adult
mime discovers a wall.   She uses the rock to knock a hole
in the wall before she is replaced by a fifth actor, an old
woman who hammers at the wall a short time, but soon tires,
goes to sleep and dies.

The realistic body of the play begins with children re-
citing nursery rhymes and playing games.   Finally, one child,
Jenny, is alone with her sister, Stephanie.   They quarrel.   Ste-

phanie says that Jenny will grow up to be an old maid "like
Mrs. Henderson." Mrs. Henderson, who lives alone, has
befriended Jenny, but does not know Stephanie. Stephanie
jealously chants, "Lady in the Corner, whose [sic] gonna
mourn ya, ashes, ashes, when you fall dead," speaking of
Mrs. Henderson.[41]

        The next scene shows Jenny and her mother shopping
for a wedding dress for Jenny. Jenny is frightened by seeing
herself in the wedding gown, and tells her mother that she
wants to call off her marriage. Her mother argues, "It's
hard to find a good man who will support you," but finally
agrees to postpone the wedding.[42]

        In the next scene, Stephanie is visiting Jenny, who is
now a bored housewife. Stephanie is a discontented student,
who is nevertheless critical of Jenny for staying at home.
Jenny next appears as a divorcee, earning her living at a
factory which is laying off women workers. Jenny discusses
organizing a strike in one scene. In the next, it is revealed
that she organized the strike, but that it failed to help the
factory workers. As the play ends, Stephanie is still a politically active student living at home with her mother, who
would like to see her marry and settle down. Jenny is home
for a visit.

        Jenny is prepared to give up on politics after her
brief foray into union work, although Stephanie challenges
her to continue her involvement. Their mother commends
them both for their courage. The play ends with a monologue
by Jenny, asking: "How long till we learn that the hand of
another in ours will give us strength?" and promising that
she "will never settle down, ... for we are in the corner no
longer."[43]

        Although the final monologue suggests a more hopeful
future, nothing in the play supports this conclusion. In the
last scene, as in the first, Stephanie and Jennifer are quarreling. While neither has "settled down," they are not independent either. Both are grown women living with their parents, although openly critical of the parents' way of life.
Jenny has rejected the life of a suburban housewife, but has
also quit her factory job, and feels that organizing the strike
was a futile gesture. She has no plans for the future, except to live at home for awhile. Stephanie is still a student,
and continues to be dissatisfied with school.

"Lady in the Corner" attempts to contrast Stephanie
and Jennifer with their mother and Mrs. Henderson, showing
that the younger women are more open to change and less
bound by convention. But the younger women's more open
attitudes do not gain them power, even over their own lives.
They are no more independent than their mother, and apparently less so than Mrs. Henderson, who at least was not
living off a man's wages as they are living off their father's.
Thus, the general impression left by the play is not one of
progress, but of circularity.   Just as in the mime that opens
the play, Stephanie and Jenny have chipped a small hole in
their wall of oppression, through which they see a vision of
autonomy.   But they are no closer to going over this wall,
transcending their oppression, than their mother was.   Stephanie and Jenny, although they are aware of their oppression, take no steps to oppose it.   They are simply the helpless victims of the socio-sexual hierarchy.

"Lady in the Corner" is like "Abide in Darkness" in
depicting an overwhelming oppression against which the protagonists do not struggle.   "Lady in the Corner," however,
attempts to tack a somewhat hopeful conclusion onto this
bleak depiction.   Because nothing in the play supports such
a hopeful conclusion, the effect is unconvincing.   The completely oppressive ending of "Abide in Darkness" is more
successful, simply because the entire, short play is directed
toward that one end.

A third example of the device of portraying women's
oppression to gain sympathy is Andrea Shepard's "Day upon
Day," performed by the Boulder Feminist Theatre. [44]   Rather
than depicting a situation that is almost universal, as "Lady
in the Corner" tries to do, "Day upon Day" focuses specifically on women in prison.   Using a realistic framework
interspersed with monologues that reveal the characters'
thoughts, "Day upon Day" shows a typical day at a women's
prison.

In the climactic scene, one of the prisoners, Hagar,
goes before the parole board.   The men on the board ask
irrelevant questions about Hagar's sex life.   They imply that
Hagar's boyfriend is a point against her release because he
has a criminal record.   However, giving him up would not
necessarily improve her chances of parole either.   When
Hagar brings up her good record of behavior in prison, the
board points out that this is not necessarily an indication of
what her behavior would be out on parole.   Finally, after a

brief, private conference, the board denies Hagar parole.
Back in the prison's day room, Hagar knocks over a table
in a fit of futile rage. Her friend, Jeanne, comforts her as
the play ends.

"Day upon Day" easily wins sympathy for the characters, because of the obvious injustice of the prison system.
Hagar is depicted in earlier scenes as a strong character,
imprisoned for stabbing a man in defense of a woman friend.
To see such a character submit passively to the incompetent
parole board reinforces the effect of overwhelming oppression; if struggle were of any use, Hagar would certainly
struggle.   Therefore, her situation must be hopeless.

In all three of these plays, the rhetorical strategy is
simply to depict an overwhelming and universal oppression,
against which it is futile for women to struggle.   The more
effectively this oppression is portrayed, the more successfully the device functions.   For this reason, "Lady in the
Corner," which is somewhat scattered in its conclusions, is
less successful than the other two plays, which concentrate
on the vivid portrayal of oppression.

Plays employing this device meet only the first part
of the definition employed in this study of feminist drama.
Although they depict an unjust socio-sexual hierarchy in the
most direct terms, they do not have a pattern of symbolic
action in which an agent seeks autonomy.   In fact, the main
characters scarcely act at all in these plays; they are acted
upon, as the pathetic victims of circumstance.

Conclusion

Four rhetorical devices can be distinguished in feminist theatre groups' productions: the sex-role reversal, the
historical role model, the satire of sexual stereotypes, and
the portrayal of women's oppression.   In general, plays employing these devices differ from the plays examined in earlier chapters in two related respects.   First, these plays
often do not follow a single agent in a pattern of action ex-
tending throughout the production.   Instead, there may be
many agents represented, enacting the symbolic pattern of
asserting their autonomy in a Readers Theatre or review
style of production.

Secondly, while most of the plays in this chapter

represent woman's goal as autonomy, many represent solidarity among women as an equally important goal, or as a
means of attaining autonomy. These two differences, both
centering on the group rather than the individual, may be
partly the result of the plays' group authorship.

A group might prefer a production in which many actors play an important role to one with a single "star," and
the importance of group solidarity would be more obvious to
them than to an individual author. The differences may also
be a result of the rather recent emphasis placed on group
solidarity in the feminist movement, and the avoidance of
movement "leaders." Although the plays in this chapter,
taken together, are not more recent than those in earlier
chapters, their authors are avowed feminists who might
follow the evolution of feminist thought more closely. Consequently, these differences may suggest, not only the limitations of the definition employed in this study, but also the
next stage of feminist drama, a new development that will
appear more clearly in the years ahead.

If the definition employed in this study is slightly
modified, it still fits the majority of the plays produced by
feminist theatre groups. All of these plays show an agent,
or agents, who represent woman seeking autonomy, often
through unity with other women, in an unjust socio-sexual
hierarchy. Those employing sex-role reversal show this
struggle in reverse, with men in the position women have
in society. This device shows that the injustice lies in the
society, rather than in woman's "naturally" inferior status.
The historical plays show women of the past struggling for
autonomy in an unjust hierarchy as an inspiration for present-
day women to emulate. The satirical plays condemn the
socio-sexual hierarchy by showing its product, the traditional
woman, and often depict such women beginning to rebel against
this hierarchy. The device lending itself least to this definition is the one that simply shows women's oppression. This
device corresponds to the first part of the definition, the depiction of an oppressive socio-sexual hierarchy. As a device, it is the most limited, since it simply establishes a
situation without showing any response. The lack of action
gives it less theatrical potential than the other devices, and
makes it best suited to short forms.

Analysis of the work of feminist theatre groups by the
definitions employed in this study reveals the common strain
in much of this work. All four of the devices discussed por-

tray an oppressive socio-sexual hierarchy. Many of the
plays also show an agent or agents opposing this hierarchy.
Those in which an agent does not oppose the hierarchy often
suggest that struggle is hopeless, and cast the blame on the
hierarchy rather than on the women characters, who are either sympathetically satirized or depicted as helpless victims.

    The use of several protagonists and the emphasis on
women's solidarity are two new strains, suggesting the possible future evolution of feminist drama. The Burkean method, because it centers on a single agent following a continuous action throughout the play, must be adapted to the analysis of such fragmentary theatrical forms. It is possible,
however, to analyze parts of such a form by this method,
and then to generalize about the themes expressed in the
parts. Thus, the method employed in this study may be
adaptable to future developments in feminist drama.

Notes

1. Patti Gillespie, "A Listing of Feminist Theatres," The-
    atre News 10 (November 1977): 22-24.

2. Interviews with Dolores Walker, Westbeth Playwrights'
    Feminist Collective, New York, New York, Decem-
    ber 1975; Dinah Leavitt, Boulder Feminist Theatre,
    Boulder, Colorado, August 1977; Ada McAllister,
    Rhode Island Feminist Theatre, in Columbia, Mis-
    souri, November 1977; Judy Sarver, B & O Theatre,
    in Columbia, Missouri, November 1977. Response
    to written questions taped by Cynthia A. Ferguson,
    Circle of the Witch, Minneapolis, Minnesota, Novem-
    ber 1977. All of those interviewed also supplied
    press clippings, publicity releases, and programs,
    on which some of the following information is based.

3. Patricia Horan, "Restaurant Blackout," and Dolores
    Walker and A. Piotrowski, "The Pick Up Schtick,"
    in the author's collection of unpublished review ma-
    terial by the Westbeth Playwrights' Feminist Collec-
    tive. Both of these skits are under two pages in
    length; therefore, page numbers are not indicated
    when they are quoted.

4. Sally Ordway, "Family, Family," in the author's collec-
    tion of unpublished review material by the Westbeth
    Playwrights' Feminist Collective.

5. Ibid., p. 57.

6. Ibid., p. 58.

7. Ibid., p. 57.

8. Myrna Lamb, "But What Have You Done for Me Late-
    ly?" in The Mod Donna and Scyklon Z: Plays of
    Women's Liberation (New York: Pathfinder Press,
    1971), pp. 143-166.

9. Ibid., p. 161.

10. Ibid., p. 151.

11. Rhode Island Feminist Theatre, The Johnnie Show,
    Shubert Playbook Series, vol. 4, no. 2.

12. Ibid., p. 4.

13. Ibid., p. 12.

14. Ibid., p. 53.

15. Ibid., p. 11.

16. Circle of the Witch, "Time Is Passing," described in
    unpublished materials in the author's collection.

17. The B & O, "30," described by Judy Sarver in the in-
    terview cited earlier.

18. Westbeth Playwrights' Feminist Collective, "Jumpin'
    Salty," 1975, description based on the interview with
    Dolores Walker cited earlier, parts of the script,
    and press releases and clippings in the collection of
    the author.

19. Rhode Island Feminist Theatre, "Anne Hutchinson:
    Rhode Island's First Independent Woman," adapted to
    video by Brandon French and Ada McAllister, 1977.

20. Anna Rudinitsky, a letter to the Women's Trade Union
    League, 1912, quoted in the program of "Time Is
    Passing" by the Circle of the Witch.

21. Linda Kline, "The Laundry Workers Present Hatpin

Bessie," in the author's collection of unpublished material by the Westbeth Playwrights' Feminist Collective.

22. Rhode Island Feminist Theatre, "Anne Hutchinson," p. 15.

23. Ibid., p. 27.

24. Ibid., p. 10.

25. Ibid., p. 6.

26. Ibid., p. 23.

27. Ibid., p. 42.

28. Interview with Judy Sarver cited earlier.

29. Terry Kennedy, "Not Just Clowning Around," Patriot Ledger, 1977, exact date not given, clipping in the author's collection.

30. Boulder Feminist Theatre, "The Boyfriend," described by Dinah Leavitt in the interview cited earlier.

31. Westbeth Playwrights' Feminist Collective, "?!," in the author's collection of unpublished materials.

32. Circle of the Witch, "Sexpot Follies," June 1974, in the author's collection of unpublished materials.

33. Susan Yankowitz, "The Chicken," in the author's collection of unpublished material from the Westbeth Playwrights' Feminist Collective.

34. Circle of the Witch, "Sexpot Follies," p. 1.

35. Ibid., p. 8.

36. Ibid., p. 15.

37. Ibid., pp. 5-6.

38. Dolores Walker, "Abide in Darkness," 1971, in the author's collection of unpublished material by the Westbeth Playwrights' Feminist Collective.

39. Ibid., p. 4.

40. Circle of the Witch, "Lady in the Corner," February,
     1975, in the author's collection of unpublished material.

41. Ibid., p. 5.

42. Ibid., p. 9.

43. Ibid., p. 26.

44. Andrea Shepard, "Day upon Day," The Second Wave,
     Summer 1974, pp. 28-37.

Chapter 7

FOR COLORED GIRLS WHO HAVE CONSIDERED
SUICIDE/WHEN THE RAINBOW IS ENUF

Introduction

Like many of the plays by feminist theatre groups,
For Colored Girls Who Have Considered Suicide/When the
Rainbow Is Enuf* by Ntozake Shange has several protagonists rather than one. Like them it is unified thematically
rather than by an extended line of action. Just as the work
of feminist theatre groups often does, For Colored Girls
represents women's support of one another as essential to
women's achievement of autonomy. For Colored Girls was
a collaborative effort like the work of feminist theatre groups,
incorporating not only Shange's verse but also her friends'
choreography, arrangements, performances and direction
from its inception to its opening on Broadway. For Colored
Girls is, however, richer in associations, more complex in
its rhetorical strategy, and certainly more popularly successful than any of the plays produced by feminist theatre groups
have been.

It is included here as an example of the level of
sophistication feminist drama has so far reached, both in
feminist philosophy and in rhetorical sophistication. Its clusters of associations depict not only the present, unjust socio-
sexual hierarchy but also an envisioned non-hierarchical society. Its pattern of symbolic action shows women interacting
as agents to transcend the unjust hierarchy. Consequently,
it is also the most thoroughly idealistic of the plays examined.

Biography

Ntozake Shange was born October 18, 1948, in Tren-

---

*For Colored Girls Who Have Considered Suicide/When the
Rainbow Is Enuf, by Ntozake Shange (New York: Macmillan,
Inc., 1977). Quotes from this play reprinted by permission.

ton, New Jersey. Her family moved several times during
her childhood, to New York State, to Missouri, and to Ala-
bama. Shange graduated from Barnard College and received
a master's degree from the University of Southern California.
Her father, Dr. Paul T. Williams, is a surgeon and her
mother, Eloise Williams, is a psychiatric social worker.

Shange's parents named her Paulette Williams but
she has legally adopted an African name. "Ntozake" means
"she who comes with her own things" and "Shange" means
"one who walks like a lion."[1] She changed her name because "I had a violent, violent resentment of carrying a slave
name; poems and music come from the pit of myself and the
pit of myself wasn't a slave."[2]

Shange grew up in a well-to-do, intellectual environment. She became an omnivorous reader at an early age:

> I read all the Russians in English (my goal in life
> was to free Raskolnikov from his guilts) and the
> French in French and the Spaniards with the aid
> of dictionaries. Simone de Beauvoir, Melville,
> Carson McCullers and Edna Millay. And Jean
> Genet. I would say to my mother that I didn't
> understand a word he was saying but I liked him. [3]

When Shange finished college, she moved to New York, no
longer financially supported by her parents. The shock of
moving from the rarefied atmosphere of home and school to
the situation of a poor black woman in Harlem was tremen-
dous. One of the poems in For Colored Girls, "a nite with
beau willie brown," was directly inspired by her experience
in Harlem. She recalls:

> It was hot. I was broke. I didn't have enough
> money for a subway token. I was miserable. The
> man in the next room was beating up his old lady.
> It went on for hours and hours. She was scream-
> ing. He was laughing. Every time he hit her I
> would think, yeah, man, well that had already hap-
> pened to me. So I sat down and wrote 'Beau Wil-
> lie.' All my anger came out. [4]

Shange's writing is frequently an expression of emotional pain. Since the age of nineteen when she was unhap-
pily married to a law student, she has attempted suicide
several times. The title of her play, For Colored Girls Who

Have Considered Suicide/When the Rainbow Is Enuf, came to
her after she had moved to California where she taught college courses. Driving home from a class one evening, she
saw a huge rainbow over Oakland. Shange realized then that
women can survive if they decide that they "have as much
right and as much purpose for being here as air and moun-
tains do. We form the same stuff here that sunlight does,
we are the same as the sky, we are here, breathing, living
creatures and we have a right to everything."[5]

    In California, Shange entered the Women's Studies
program at Sonoma State College. The courses she took
there, Shange has commented,

> are inextricably bound to the development of my
> sense of the world, myself, and women's language.
> Studying the mythology of women from antiquity to
> the present day led directly to the piece "Sechita"
> in For Colored Girls in which a dance hall girl is
> perceived as deity, as slut, as innocent and know-
> ing. Unearthing the mislaid, forgotten, &/or mis-
> understood women writers, painters, mothers, cow-
> girls, and union leaders of our pasts proved to be
> both a supportive experience and a challenge not
> to let them down, not to do less than--at all costs
> not to be less woman than--our mothers, from
> Isis to Marie Laurencin, Zora Neale Hurston to
> Käthe Kollwitz, Anna May Wong to Calamity Jane.[6]

Thus, Shange is among the first generation of writers to be
consciously influenced by the recent wave of feminist activity
in scholarship.

    For Colored Girls began as a performance of poems,
dance, and music by Shange and friends in San Francisco
Bay area bars. Shange recalls:

> I began reading my poetry in women's bars. Not
> lesbian bars, necessarily, but women's bars,
> where they can go without being hassled or having
> someone try to pick them up. Anyhow those were
> the only places that would hire me, and when I
> was there I realized I was where I belonged.[7]

The selection of poems and music changed frequently during
this period and continued to evolve when the performers took
their production to New York. Oz Scott, who became the

stage director for the New York opening, suggested final
changes to make the performance more theatrical and cohe-
sive. The New York Shakespeare Festival picked up the play
after its opening as a workshop in the Henry Street Theatre
and moved it to the Public Theatre and finally to the Booth
Theatre on Broadway.

　　For Colored Girls opened on Broadway in September
of 1976 to popular acclaim. While most critics praised the
play, a minority saw it as an exploitation of audience sympathy for blacks and women. Stanley Kauffmann commented:

> Most of the pieces seemed to me hyperdramatic
> and--as writing--superficial, given occasional
> weight by some skill in presentation and of course
> by the extra-poetic, extra-theatrical pressure of
> the subject. That subject is what it's like to grow
> up black and female in the U. S. [8]

Following the success of For Colored Girls, Joseph Papp
commissioned a new play from Shange for the New York
Shakespeare Festival. A Photograph: A Still Life with
Shadows/A Photograph: A Study of Cruelty opened at the
Lu Esther Hall/Public Theatre in December of 1977. Oz
Scott was again director and the cast included some actors
from For Colored Girls.

　　Photograph was not as successful as Shange's first
play either critically or in the length of its run. Richard
Eder summed up the critical response in his New York
Times review:

> Miss Shange is something besides a poet but she
> is not--at least not at this stage--a dramatist.
> More than anything else she is a troubadour. She
> declares her fertile vision of the love and pain be-
> tween black women and black men in outbursts full
> of old malice and young cheerfulness.... But the
> work is forced, and finally broken by its form.
> The perceptions are made to do the donkeywork of
> holding up what attempts to be a whole dramatic
> structure, and they fail. [9]

　　David Murray provided music for Photograph as well
as for an off-Broadway play, "Where the Mississippi Meets
the Amazon," in which Shange was a writer and performer.
In July of 1977, Shange formalized her three-year relation-

ship with Murray before their family and friends, although
without a civil or religious ceremony.

In December of 1977, Shange commented about the
success of For Colored Girls: "I still live mainly the way
I always lived. Have the same friends. Do the same things.
What Colored Girls did do was make it possible for me to
visit Paris without marrying a rich man."[10] In the introduction to For Colored Girls, Shange writes: "i am on the
other side of the rainbow/picking up the pieces of days spent
waitin for the poem to be heard/while you listen/i have other
work to do."[11]

Plot Summary

The opening lines in For Colored Girls, spoken by
"the lady in brown," state the play's purpose:

> somebody/anybody
> sing a black girl's song
> bring her out
> . . . .
> sing the song of her possibilities (p. 2)

Each of the seven black actresses then speaks, the first one
saying, "i'm outside chicago," the next "i'm outside detroit,"
and so on until they have all named an American city. The
lady in brown completes the opening sequence by saying "&
this is for colored girls who have considered:suicide/but
moved to the ends of their own:rainbows." (p. 3)

The actresses begin the play's second section by singing children's songs and games. These continue into longer
statements about growing up, entering dance contests, high
school graduation, and sexual initiation. The third section
begins with a statement entitled, "no assistance." The
speaker is the lady in red, who addresses a man she has
loved "assiduously for 8 months 2 wks & a day," as "an
experiment/to see ... if I waz capable of debasin my self
for the love of another/if I cd stand not being wanted/ ... &
I cannot." (p. 10) This section continues with a stark statement on rape and another on abortion.

The next several poems create more detailed charac-
terizations of individual black women. "Sechita" portrays a
black dance hall girl with her roots in "quadroon balls/ele-

gance in st. louis" and even more ancient ones in the "egyptian goddess of creativity/2nd millenium." (p. 18) Despite her "stockings darned wit yellow thread" and her "gin-stained garters," Sechita is defiant, kicking "viciously thru the nite/catchin stars tween her toes." In another poem, a black girl is growing up in a newly integrated St. Louis neighborhood in the fifties. Instead of reading children's books at the library, she discovers Toussaint L'Ouverture, the Haitian rebel, in books from the adult reading room. Eventually she runs away from home with Toussaint as her imaginary companion. A third poem in this section portrays a woman who dresses in silk roses and aqua sequins, wanting to be "a memory/a wound to every man/arrogant enough to want her." (p. 25) She lures the men home with her for sexual encounters, then throws them out, "vengeful," before morning, and cries herself to sleep.

The next section begins with a poem entitled "i used to live in the world." In it, the lady in blue begins by describing her experience of oppression in Harlem: "i hadda right to the world: then i moved to Harlem." (p. 30) She goes on to comfort other women who are the victims of harassment as she is:

> never mind sister
> dont pay him no mind
> go go go go go go sister
> do yr thing
> never mind (p. 30)

In "pyramid," three women overcome their rivalrous interest in the same man when they discover the "love between them: love like sisters." (p. 33) A series of direct statements follows in which all the women address their lovers, asking to "lemme love you just like i am," and culminating in the group dancing while chanting a sequence that begins, "my love is too delicate to have thrown back in my face." (p. 35)

The suspenseful climax of the play comes in a poem entitled "a nite with beau willie brown." Beau Willie, back from Vietnam, is hiding out from the police in his home town where his two children live with Crystal, their mother. Crystal, now twenty-two and self supporting, has been Beau Willie's "girl" since she was thirteen. After Beau Willie beat her and the children, she got a court order forbidding him to come to their home. In the poem, Beau Willie goes to the apartment to make up with Crystal. Crystal locks him

out of the apartment, so he breaks in, and eventually coaxes
Crystal into letting him hold the children. When he has them,
he holds them out the fifth-story window, threatening to drop
them unless Crystal promises to marry him. Before she can
speak, he lets the children drop.

     The final section of the play, in which all the actresses
participate, is entitled, "a layin on of hands." It begins,
"i waz missing somethin," something that is "free," "pure,"
that is not "layin on bodies" or "mama/holdin me tight" but
a haunting need, "the ghost of another woman/who waz missin
what I waz missin." (pp. 48-50) The resolution comes when
the last speaker, the lady in red, describes being caught up
and cradled by the trees, the moon, and the sky. All the
actresses say and then sing the words, "i found god in myself: & i loved her: i loved her fiercely." (p. 51) The
actresses "enter into a closed tight circle" and the play ends
with the lady in brown saying again, "& this is for colored
girls who have considered:suicide/but are movin to the end
of their own:rainbows." (p. 51)

Associational Clusters

     Two primary associational clusters appear in the poems
that comprise For Colored Girls. One cluster associates
the dirt and loneliness of cities on the sensory level, the
isolation of the technological society on the abstract level,
and the oppression of black women by black men on the familial level. Opposing this cluster is one that associates
singing, dancing, and natural beauty on the sensory level,
relationships of equality between men and women on the familial level, and a mythological, non-Christian spirituality
on the abstract level. The two clusters create a contrast
on all three levels of meaning between the reality of the
present, oppressive hierarchy and an envisioned society in
which a natural order would prevail permitting women's full
human development.

     The association between isolation and technology is
first made in "abortion cycle #1." The speaker describes
her isolated situation: "i cdnt have my friends see this ...
this hurts me: & nobody came: cuz nobody knew: once i
was pregnant and shamed of myself." (p. 17) Her situation
is described in terms of "tubes tables ... metal horses
gnawin my womb ... steel rods," all representing the sterile
and disapproving technological society. In a later poem, the

connection between sterility and the white male-dominated
society is reinforced:

> we deal wit emotion too much
> so why dont we go on ahead & be white then
> & make everythin dry & abstract wit no rhythm & no
> reelin for sheer sensual pleasure (p. 35)

Finally the speaker drops her ironic tone to condemn such
abstraction as "empty."

The oppressive society which evolves from these associations is distinctly urban.   In "i used to live in the world,"
Harlem is described as "ol men's bodies: shit & broken lil
whiskey bottles: left to make me bleed." (p. 28)   In such
a world, "i can ride anywhere: remaining a stranger," (p.
29) not only isolated but continually threatened, continually
hoping to elude the attention of men.   The oppressor might
be almost anyone, "a tall short black brown young man fulla
his power," (p. 29) aware of his privileged position in the
socio-sexual hierarchy.

Another poem, "latent rapists'," adds that the rapist
might even be an acquaintance of the victim, "these men
friends of ours: who smile nice: stay employed: and take
us out to dinner." (p. 14)   If such an acquaintance should
rape a woman, she will find it hard to press charges since
the societal stereotype indicates that "a rapist is always to
be a stranger: to be legitimate: someone you never saw:
a man wit obvious problems." (p. 13)   Ironically, the same
society persuades these male acquaintances of their power
and of the relative safety of committing such a rape.   The
men know that society's reasoning will be: "if you know
him: you must have wanted it." (p. 12)   In this cluster the
urban isolation of a technological society is an instrument
of women's oppression.   Their bodies are depersonalized,
available for exploitation even by "friends" who know they
are safe from accusations.

Opposing this cluster is one of natural beauty, spirituality, song and dance.   In "i usedta live in the world," the
speaker contrasts the two clusters using images of water:

> when i walked in the pacific
> i imagined waters ancient from accra/tunis
> cleansin me/feedin me
> now my ankles are coated in grey filth
> from the puddle neath the hydrant (p. 28)

The dirty city hydrant associated with the urban ugliness of
the hierarchical society is contrasted with the ancient beauty
of the ocean.

Similarly, the first cluster is associated with "melody-
less-ness," the second with "the song of her [black woman's]
possibilities." (p. 2)   Singing and dancing develop into complex associations as the play continues.   In the early poems,
"graduation nite" and "now i love somebody more than," in
which a black teenager goes to the Spanish district to enter
a dance contest, music and dancing are simply positive sensory images.   Eventually, dancing is revealed as a means
of coping with oppression as well: "we gotta dance to keep
from dyin." (p. 11)   The woman in orange describes how
she can "leave bitterness in somebody else's cup ... when
i can dance like that/theres nothin cd hurt me." (p. 33)

Later in the play, the association of music and dance
with religious myth, first made in the opening reference to
singing a righteous gospel, is further developed.   The lady
in purple describes how, before she fell in love and became
vulnerable to a man, she "lived wit myths & music waz my
old man & i cd dance: a dance outta time." (p. 34)   Sechita
also lives with myths, using dance to defy her situation:

> her calf was tauntin the brazen carnie
> lights/the full moon/sechita/goddess of love/egypt
> second millenium/performin the rites/the conjurin
>   of men
> conjurin the spirit (p. 19)

Although Sechita thinks of herself as performing spiritual
rites, these rites have nothing to do with Christianity.   She
identifies herself with an Egyptian goddess and with the moon,
and is anxious to leave dusty Natchez where a male "god
seemed to be wipin his feet in her face." (p. 19)   Since the
moon is often associated with the worship of female deities,
both a nature religion and a matriarchal religion are suggested.

Similarly, in a later poem the lady in yellow says,
"my spirit is too ancient to understand the separation of
soul & gender." (p. 36)   Thus, the spirituality that develops
in the play is non-Christian, perhaps pre-Christian, a goddess
religion that does not separate body and soul either to oppress women or to condemn sexuality, but one in which "god-
liness is plenty is ripe & fertile." (p. 35)

This cluster of associations also includes the recognition of black women's natural physical beauty contrasted with its suppression in the dominant culture. Black women's appearance is first referred to in the play's opening statement, in which the lady in brown says that "the black girl ... doesn't know the sound: of her own voice: her infinite beauty." (p. 2) In "Sechita," the societal condemnation of black woman's appearance is parodied in the description of Sechita's mirror:

> the broken mirror she
> used to decorate her face/made her forehead tilt
>   backwards/
> her cheeks appear sunken/her sassy chin only
>   large enuf/
> to keep her full lower lip/from growin into her
>   neck/sechita/
> had learned to make allowances for the distortions
>   (p. 18)

Sechita's mirror is the mirror of society, distorting the black woman's appearance even in her own eyes to that of a Neanderthal type with sloping forehead, giant lips and no chin. The defiant Sechita knows better than to believe this distorted picture of herself thrown back by the "broken mirror" of society.

The lady who wears "orange butterflies & acqua sequins" uses these false values of beauty against the men who hold them, wreaking a pathetic vengeance for herself and other women. She attracts attention with "Rhinestones etchin the corners of her mouth," "pastel ivy drawn on her shoulders." (p. 25) When she has had sex with one of the men she attracts with her dress and makeup, she rises and bathes to "remove his smell: to wash away the glitter." (p. 26) In the bath she becomes "herself: ordinary: brown braided woman: with big legs & full hips." (p. 26) Then she awakens her lover and tells him to go home so she can work. The men now see in her a "reglar colored girl: fulla the same malice: livid indifference as a sistah: worn from supportin a wd be hornplayer: or waitin by the window: & they knew: & left in a hurry." (p. 27) She has proven to herself once again that her real, black self is not interesting to these men who are only attracted by rhinestones and feathers.

Thus, the two clusters of associations contrast black

women's real but often unrecognized beauty with the view society, including black men, often holds of black women: that
they are physically unattractive unless they are decked in
rhinestones or can-can skirts to hide their natural appearance.

   "I used to live in the world" adds a further twist to
the "metaphysical dilemma" the black woman faces. While
a black woman's natural beauty will not usually be recognized,
she may be endangered if it is:

>   i come in at dusk
>   stay close to the curb
>   round midnite
>   praying wont no young man
>   think i'm pretty in a dark mornin (p. 29)

Particularly in the sordid, urban environment of Harlem, a
woman who is attractive or even friendly is asking for the
attention of rapists and molesters: "reglar beauty & a smile
in the street: is just a set-up." (p. 30)

   In For Colored Girls, the natural physical and spiritual beauty of black women is associated with the beauty of
nature. The lady in purple describes herself when she is
rejected by her lover as "ready to die like a lily in the
desert." (p. 35) Her rejection, apparently, is caused in
part by her lack of socially approved "beauty," a lack she
ruefully describes: "Here/: is what i have/: poems/ big
thighs/lil tits/ &: so much love/will you take it from me
this one time." (p. 35)

   In the final poem, "a layin on of hands," direct associations are made among black women's self image, the
beauty of nature, and a non-Christian spirituality. The term,
"laying on of hands," suggests a religious gesture of blessing
and healing. The lady in purple says that the laying on of
hands will be "the holiness of myself released," (p. 50) im-
plying a spirituality based on self respect. Nature offers the
women comfort in a tree that "took me up in her branches:
held me in the breeze: made me dawn dew: that chill at
daybreak: the sun wrapped me up swingin rose light every-
where." (p. 50) Finally, all of these elements resolve in
the final song, "i found god in myself" and the statement
following: "& this is for colored girls who have considered:
suicide/but are moving to the ends of their own: rainbows."
(p. 51)

The beauty of nature, represented in the rainbow, comforts the women and enables them to begin to love themselves. The final poem and song suggest a goddess worship that is partly self acceptance and sororal love, partly an experience of transcendent nature.

Thus the two primary clusters of associations in For Colored Girls form a series of contrasts on all three levels of meaning. In one cluster, the present reality of the unjust socio-sexual hierarchy is associated with urban ugliness on the sensory level, with the impersonality of technological society on the abstract level, and with the rejection of black women's true beauty and their exploitation and harassment by men of their own race on the familial level. In the opposing cluster, a society is envisioned in which black women's true beauty would be recognized by men and by other women, and in which "soul & gender" would not be separated, a society reflected in matriarchal myth and in the transcendent beauty of nature.

Pattern of Symbolic Action

Although For Colored Girls has many protagonists rather than one, a pattern of symbolic action emerges in the play to which the central figures in each succeeding poem contribute. The poem that opens the play reflects this pattern of symbolic action in miniature, showing black women's struggle for and achievement of autonomy. In this first poem as in the entire play, the pattern begins with a statement of black women's struggle for survival against desperate odds. The poem goes on as the play will to describe the individual acts of hopeless defiance black women have historically performed. The oppressiveness of their situation is explored and a more hopeful response based on sisterhood and self respect develops. After a final, almost despairing moment, both the initial poem and the play itself resolve optimistically in a vision of a non-hierarchical, spiritually integrated future for black women.

The first poem follows this pattern of action largely through associations with song and dance both positive and negative. In the opening words, black women's desperate situation is described: "it's funny/it's hysterical: the melody-less-ness of her dance ... she's dancin on beer cans & shingles." (p. 1) The poem continues by elaborating on individuals' vain attempts to alter this situation. Once again,

the action is expressed in musical associations: "another
song with no singers: Lyrics/no voices: & interrupted
solos: unseen performances." (p. 1)

The lines that follow suggest the depth of black wom-
en's oppression: "i can't hear anythin: but maddening
screams: & the soft strains of death." (p. 2) A more hopeful response begins to emerge in the poem's exhortation:
"sing a black girl's song: bring her out." (p. 2) After a
final, almost despairing note: "she's been dead so long:
closed in silence so long," the poem resolves in an optimistic
call: "sing the song of her possibilities: sing a righteous
gospel: let her be born." (p. 2)

The arrangement of poems that constitutes the entire
play's pattern of action reflects the same progression as this
opening poem: a general statement of black women's oppression; individual efforts in the past to defy this oppression;
an exploration in depth of the nature of the oppression; a
suggestion of hope followed by a moment of despair and a
final, spiritual affirmation of black women's eventual autonomy.

The initial statement of black women's desperate
struggle for autonomy in the play, like that in the first poem,
is found in the act of dancing. Like the dancing "on beer
cans & shingles," the dancing in "graduation nite" and "now
i love somebody more than" is a metaphor for black wom-
en's struggle to grow up, survive, and attain autonomy. The
young women in these two poems use dancing to assert their
maturity: "i waz the only virgin: so i hadda make like my
hips waz into some business." (p. 6) Music and dance are
also a defiance of the white hierarchical system, reflected
in such lines as: "if jesus cdnt play a horn like shepp/
waznt no need for colored folks to bear no cross at all."
(p. 9) These attempts to achieve adulthood and autonomy
end, however, in the statements on rape and abortion representing the obstacles these exuberant young women will face.

The second phase of the play shows "interrupted
solos: unseen performances"--the vain attempts of heroic
individuals to defy their oppressive situations. Sechita,
trapped in the tawdry life of the carnival, imagines herself
a priestess. The men who come to yell and throw coins at
her are men she has conjured by the full moon. Her courage and pride are remarkable, but neither this nor any re-

sponse can alter her situation. Similarly, the woman in sequins and rhinestones turns men's impersonal attempts to exploit her against them by treating them just as impersonally. But her efforts only sadden her and do not seriously wound her lovers. In "Toussaint," a little black girl defies her situation by running away from home, inspired by the history of Toussaint L'Ouverture. But when she reaches the waterfront and meets a real little boy named Toussaint, she drops her defiant attempt to escape, resigning herself to reality with the aid of her new friend. The symbolic actions in this section of the play all show the courage and the hopelessness of individual women's acts of defiance against the unjust hierarchy.

Just as the opening poem of the play next plumbs the depths of women's oppression in "maddening screams: & the soft strains of death," so the play itself explores this oppression in "i used to live in the world," in which the speaker's actions are restricted to coming in at dusk, staying close to the curb and praying not to attract the attention of any man. In this same poem, however, the first ray of hope appears. The act of offering sympathy to a similarly oppressed woman--"never mind sister: dont pay him no mind" (p. 30)--is the first in a series of gestures towards women's solidarity.

The next poem develops this action in the story of three friends with "one laugh: one music: one flowered shawl: knotted on each neck." (p. 31) Although all three are attracted to the same man, they allow him to choose one of them; then the other two avoid him. When after his repeated attempts to attract these two, they finally succumb to him, it is the turn of the friend chosen first to forgive them. She does so, "understandin how much love stood between them." (p. 33) The line is nicely ambiguous, suggesting both the love the women feel toward each other and their attraction to the same man, an attraction that creates a barrier to love among the women. All three women take positive action to help one another and to preserve the love between them. This assertion of a difficult and beautiful love among women, even those competing for the same man, strengthens the speakers in the next section to assert themselves.

In the series, "no more love poems," each speaker individually asserts her need to be respected, ending in the choral sequence, "my love is too delicate to have thrown back

in my face." The sharing of expressions of self respect develops into a group dance with chanting and clapping until
"the dance reaches a climax and all of the ladies fall out
tired, but full of life and togetherness." (p. 39)   The acts
of sharing continue as each of the women relates her favorite
male excuse for having hurt her:

> lady in yellow: get this, last week my ol man
>   came in sayin, 'i don't know how
>   she got yr number baby, i'm sorry'
> lady in brown: no this one is it, 'o baby, ya know
>   i waz high, i'm sorry' (p. 41)

The sequence is suggestive of a lively consciousness-raising
group in which each individual recognizes the societal quality
of her oppression.

A final despairing note is struck in the play, just as
in the opening poem's line, "she's been dead so long," in
"a nite with beau willie brown." Significantly, the woman
in this story, Crystal, is completely isolated throughout the
poem. The narrator, who seems at first to be a sympathetic
observer, turns out in a sudden revelation at the end of the
poem to be Crystal herself. The only other woman mentioned is the "bartendin bitch at the merry-go-round cafe"
on whom Beau Willie has been spending all his money. Because Crystal is completely alone, she is vulnerable. Beau
Willie finally persuades her to give him the children because
he "oozed kindness &: crystal who had known so lil/let beau
hold kwame." (p. 47) Because she has no "sisters" to de-
pend on, she looks hopelessly for kindness from the oppressor,
unable to survive in total isolation.

After this bleak moment, the play's final symbolic action is a search by all the women for "a layin on of hands:
the holiness of myself released." The search is communal,
the poem's lines spoken by each of the women in turn. Because of this, and because each woman is aware of "the
ghost of another woman who waz missin what i waz missin,"
the play ends in an affirmation of women's spiritual autonomy:
"i found god in myself: & i loved her fiercely." (p. 51)

Thus, the pattern of symbolic action in For Colored
Girls is one of black women's struggle for autonomy against
the racist, sexist hierarchy. Conducted individually, this
struggle is one of desperate courage doomed to failure. But
with the support of other women, an autonomy becomes pos-

sible that is not only psychological or societal but spiritual
as well.

Agent:Scene Ratio

Although For Colored Girls has many protagonists
rather than one, its pattern of symbolic action is clearly a
search for autonomy opposed by an unjust socio-sexual hierarchy. The search for autonomy in For Colored Girls succeeds, however, more thoroughly than in any of the other
plays studied. Thus, it is the most idealistic of the plays
examined as well.

The successful resolution to the search for autonomy
is attributable first to the communal nature of the struggle.
For Colored Girls has many agents who share in the same
struggle, but just as significantly, none of these agents is
able to transcend the unjust hierarchy alone. Rather the
play's pattern of symbolic action shows a progression of sympathetic sharing and support among women culminating in the
communal recitation and singing that ends the play.

Secondly, the play's optimistic resolution results from
the agents' affirmations of self building through the play.
The colored girl who at the beginning of the play "doesn't
know the sound of her own voice: her infinite beauty," affirms by the end of the play that she has found God in herself. These two elements in the achievement of autonomy,
sisterhood and self realization, are symbolically united in
the final song which affirms the holiness of self and which
is sung by the whole community of women onstage.

Finally, the achievement of autonomy in For Colored
Girls is not only socio-sexual or psychological but spiritual
as well. The spirituality of the play's resolution, reflected
in images of blessing hands, the spirits of women of the past
haunting present-day women and the female god women find
in themselves suggests the spiritual transcendence of sexism
described by Mary Daly in Beyond God the Father. Such a
transcendence, Daly says, will be "an ontological, spiritual
revolution, pointing beyond the idolatries of sexist society
and sparking creative action in and toward transcendence."[12]

Just as Daly describes, the agents in For Colored
Girls confront their own "non-being" in the fact of their "non-
existence" as persons in the unjust hierarchy. Sechita has

learned to disbelieve the grotesque distortion which is society's reflected image of her.   The lady in sequins and feathers understands that without her costume she is nothing to
the men who court her.   The woman who lives in Harlem
knows that she has no right to live and move freely in the
world.

        As Daly suggests, this ontological confrontation with
non-being is a transforming experience for the agents in the
play.   The transformation of the women comes when their
consciousness is raised, when they understand that they are
non-beings because they are women and that this non-being
is shared by all women.   As the women in For Colored Girls
recognize the communal nature of their oppression they gain
strength or, Daly would say, they gain an energy source:

> The moving center which is the energy source of
> the new sisterhood ... is the promise in ourselves.
> It is the promise in our foremothers whose history
> we are beginning to discover, and in our sisters
> whose voices have been stolen from them.   Our
> journey is the fruit of this promise--a journey into
> individualization and participation, leaving behind
> the false self and sexist society. [13]

In the play, as in Daly's description, the discovery of wom-
en's community leads to a spiritual transcendence of the sexist society in a recognition of each individual's self worth.

        Because of this recognition of individual worth, no
one is sacrificed in reaching the optimistic resolution of For
Colored Girls.   The unjust socio-sexual hierarchy is not destroyed but transcended.   As the lady in blue says:

> one thing i don' need
> is any more apologies
> . . . .
> i'm gonna do exactly what i want to
> & i wont be sorry for none of it (p. 42)

There are to be no more scapegoats, either victims of the
hierarchy or those who have profited from it now punished.
Instead, women will end the hierarchy by refusing to be victims, by doing what they want with their lives.   God is a
process within each individual, not a guilt-inducing father in
heaven nor a suffering scapegoat expiating the sins of all.
Consequently, women can support one another in transcending

the unjust hierarchy and establishing a new, non-hierarchical order which respects the worth of each individual.

Thus, For Colored Girls is among the most idealistic of the plays studied, reflecting the feminist philosophy out-lined by Daly more fully than any of the other plays studied. As Daly does, the play goes beyond denunciation of the un-just status quo to evoke an alternative, non-hierarchical or-der based on sororal community and a recognition of the worth of each individual. In For Colored Girls the agents' affirmation of individuality and community transcends the socio-sexual hierarchy, making the play an idealistic state-ment of the feminist impulse.

Conclusion

For Colored Girls expresses a more encompassing and positive view of an alternative, non-hierarchical society than any of the other plays studied. Its clusters of associa-tions depict not only the impersonal, technological hierarchy which maintains women's "non-being," but also its opposite, a spiritually fertile society founded on mutual respect and associated with music, nature, and the physical beauty of black women.

Its pattern of symbolic action, fragmented among several agents, emerges as a continuing struggle for auton-omy. This struggle is at first carried on futilely by indivi-dual women. When the individual women unite their efforts, they succeed in transcending the unjust hierarchy, affirming the spiritual dignity of each individual. For Colored Girls is therefore among the most idealistic of the plays examined as well as the most expressive of emergent feminist spiritu-ality.

Notes

1. "Trying to Be Nice," Time, July 19, 1976, p. 44.

2. Ntozake Shange, interview in New York Times, 16 June 1976, p. 27.

3. Ntozake Shange, interview in New Yorker, 2 August 1976, p. 18.

4. Ntozake Shange, interview in <u>Time</u>, 19 July 1976, p. 45.

5. Ntozake Shange, interview in <u>New York Times</u>, 16 June 1976, p. 27.

6. Ntozake Shange, <u>For Colored Girls Who Have Considered Suicide/When the Rainbow Is Enuf</u> (New York: Macmillan Pub. Co., Inc., 1977), p. x.

7. Ntozake Shange, interview in <u>New York Times</u>, 16 December 1977, sec. C, p. 6.

8. Stanley Kauffmann, "Suite and Sour," <u>New Republic</u>, 3 July 1976, p. 21.

9. Richard Eder, "Stage: 'Photograph' by Miss Shange," <u>New York Times</u>, 22 December 1977, sec. C, p. 11.

10. Ntozake Shange, interview in <u>New York Times</u>, 16 December 1977, sec. C, p. 6.

11. Ntozake Shange, <u>For Colored Girls Who Have Considered Suicide/When the Rainbow Is Enuf</u>, p. xiv. Subsequent page references to <u>For Colored Girls</u> ... in this chapter will be in parentheses following the quotation in the text. Because Shange uses the virgule (/) as a punctuation mark within lines of her poetry, I have not employed the usual practice of using a virgule to indicate the end of a line. Instead, the end of a line will be indicated with a colon (:).

12. Mary Daly, <u>Beyond God the Father</u> (Boston: Beacon Press, 1974), p. 6.

13. <u>Ibid.</u>, p. 158.

Chapter 8

CONCLUSION

Burke's concept of the rhetorical motive has been a useful center of focus in this study. This concept unites the artistic and the political in analyzing the rhetorical strategy of a work. His method has made it possible to examine the political concept of feminism in the artistic framework of drama, without judging the form and the content as separate elements. In Burke's view the artistry of a work lies in its rhetorical strategy. Thus, in evaluating a play by this standard, one considers the artfulness of the persuasive attempt, the degree to which the rhetorical strategy encompasses the situation.

In this study the associational clusters and pattern of symbolic action suggested as tools by Burke have been employed in examining the rhetorical motives of several plays. These tools have functioned not only in revealing what the rhetorical motive in each play is, but also in demonstrating the clarity and the complexity with which that motive is expressed.

Some of the plays examined by this method, such as In the Boom Boom Room, have revealed clusters of associations interrelated on several levels. These plays are a sophisticated expression of the rhetorical motive, encompassing complex situations. In others, particularly in some of the short plays written by feminist theatre groups, a relative lack of depth and complexity in the associational clusters reflects a more simplistic expression of the same rhetorical motive. Some of the plays have revealed a pattern of symbolic action that is clearly reflective of this motive. Wine in the Wilderness, for instance, follows a single protagonist in a continuous line of action that extends throughout the play. The Bed Was Full focuses less clearly on a single agent. Its pattern of symbolic action is not so readily grasped, and the rhetorical motive is not so clearly communicated. For Colored Girls, however, maintains a clear pattern of symbolic action while employing a number of protagonists. In each case, the tools suggested by Burke for examining rhe-

torical motive have been useful in evaluating the plays, and
especially appropriate to the examination of the feminist impulse (a socio-political motive) in the drama (an artistic
form).

In the opening chapter of this study, a definition of the
feminist impulse was asserted, and cast into Burkean terms:
a feminist drama is one in which the agent, a woman, seeks
autonomy within an unjust socio-sexual hierarchy. The definition, suggested by the writing of feminist theorists, incorporates two ideas that are central to feminist thought. One,
the idea of women's powerlessness as a group in society, is
reflected in the portrayal of the unjust socio-sexual hierarchy, the society denying women power. The second is the
idea that woman is not autonomous, that she is an object,
an "other," existing only in relation to men. This idea is
portrayed in her struggle for autonomy against the oppressive
society.

The definition has been employed as a standard with
which the rhetorical motive of plays can be compared. All
literature has a rhetorical motive according to Burke. In
other words, literature attempts to persuade the audience of
its view of the world. If the play's associational clusters and
pattern of symbolic action reflect the feminist assertion of
woman's desire for autonomy in an oppressive society, the
play's rhetorical motive is feminist, and the play can be
considered a feminist drama by that standard.

This definition has been a useful point of comparison
in analyzing the plays. It has served to distinguish plays
with a feminist rhetorical motive from plays that are by and
about women, but not centrally motivated by the feminist impulse. Such an approach focuses on what is in the play itself
rather than on what might have been expected of such a playwright or of such a topic. As a result, some plays have appeared to be feminist or have appeared not to be, in contra-
diction to what popular opinion might assume. Rabe's In the
Boom Boom Room, for instance, written by a man and set in
a go-go bar, reveals a feminist rhetorical motive in its associations and pattern of symbolic action. Tina Howe's Birth
and After Birth, written by a woman, set in a suburban
home, and anthologized as "women's theatre," does not.

The definition has also functioned to reveal an underlying similarity in plays with obvious stylistic differences.
The similarity is apparent both in the plays by individual

playwrights and in those by feminist theatre groups. The farcical, non-realistic style of The Bed Was Full, and the realistic, serious style of Wine in the Wilderness are widely disparate. Yet the plays are similar in portraying a woman's struggle for autonomy against her society's attempts to force her into objectified, stereotypical roles.

Plays with several agents, such as For Colored Girls and some of the plays by feminist theatre groups, still reveal a feminist motive by portraying women struggling for autonomy against an oppressive society. These plays, however, move beyond Burke's single scapegoat as agent, reflecting the feminist spirituality described by Mary Daly in her Beyond God the Father. Their use of a fragmentary, thematic organization enables these plays to emphasize the universality of women's oppression. For Colored Girls goes on to reflect the ideal of a feminist, non-hierarchical community. Thus, although the definition based on Burke's theory is limited by its focus on a single agent following a continuous line of action, it has still proven to be a useful standard by which to evaluate and compare all the plays considered.

While most of the plays examined share a feminist rhetorical motive, they differ not only in style but in how they express this motive. Thus, each play focuses on a certain aspect of the oppressive society. Each deals with this oppression with a different degree of complexity. Different plays show the agent succeeding or failing in the achievement of autonomy to different degrees. Because the degree to which agent or scene dominates indicates the philosophical school to which the play is allied, the agent's success or failure shows whether the play is idealistic or materialistic in its philosophy. Although these plays share the same rhetorical motive, they also demonstrate the depth and breadth of expression that the feminist impulse has inspired.

The least realistic, most farcical extreme of feminist drama represented is The Bed Was Full. These qualities enable it to depict the unjust socio-sexual hierarchy clearly, but restrict its depiction of the agent's struggle for autonomy. The play's lack of a rational sequence of events permits the representation of society's many limiting demands. In a more realistic environment, such demands are made more subtly and over a lifetime, and would be more difficult to represent onstage. But in the irrational world of this play, male characters can demand a profusion of roles in quick sequence, ordering Kali to play the role of mother, of servant, of mistress, of muse, without needing a rationale for such a multiplicity of demands. Because the characters speak in the clichéd language of bedroom farce, their demands have a familiar ring, bearing a resemblance to society's demands despite their non-realistic setting.

Thus, the non-realistic style of The Bed Was Full is appropriate to the depiction of sexual stereotyping, and the play succeeds in portraying this aspect of women's oppression humorously and effectively. Although it does not examine the roots of the oppression, it shows the pervasive, universal quality of such stereotyping very well. The play succeeds less well in portraying a clear pattern of symbolic action. Although Kali, the agent, does resist the demands placed on her, the play represents her resistance as fleetingly as it does each of the stereotypes. The emphasis is on maintaining the quick, comic rhythm, without pausing to place special emphasis on Kali's actions. She is the central character, if only because she participates actively in nearly every episode, while all the other characters are offstage for parts of the play. But the development of her symbolic action is somewhat submerged in the frenzied, comic activity that characterizes the play.

The Bed Was Full is typical of comedy in that it ends with a restoration of order and the pairing up of all the characters. Critics such as Susanne Langer and Northrop Frye would say that this restoration of society is a defining characteristic of comedy. However, the society at the end of The Bed Was Full is not a new and more perfect one. If anything, it is somewhat worse. Kali, who was a paid artist's model at the beginning of the play, is forced offstage at gunpoint to be another man's unpaid model at the end. Her situation seems, if not more oppressive, at least more graphically stated in this ironic pairing up of kidnapper and victim at the close of the play.

Because agent is defeated by scene at the end of The Bed Was Full, it is allied to the materialistic, deterministic philosophy. Its determinism is somewhat weakened, however, by the sporadic quality of Kali's resistance. It is difficult to determine whether the oppressive hierarchy, pervasive as it is represented to be, might not yet be overcome by a stronger agent than Kali. Thus, the play's pessimism is not completely convincing.

In the Boom Boom Room, in contrast, depicts an
agent struggling violently against her oppression, and yet
being defeated, creating a more completely deterministic impact. This play presents the most complex picture of the
oppressive society, and reaches the most pessimistic conclusion of any of the plays examined. The clusters of associations build and interrelate to depict a society of mounter and
mounted, founded on the paternal relationship and enforced by
violence. The world of go-go bars becomes a metaphor for
society in its grim, sexual exploitation of woman. The many
levels on which the oppression appears touch on the roots of
sexism and also on its more subtle aspects in realistic style.
Essentially, the play suggests that sexism, like racism, is
motivated by fear of the other, fear that the oppressed will
become the oppressor if permitted even a first step toward
autonomy.

Against this monolithic hierarchy, the agent, Chrissy,
struggles more and more violently and consciously for her
autonomy. Because the play is serious and realistic in style,
the audience can perceive this struggle to be in earnest, as
they may not with a play like The Bed Was Full. Finally,
Chrissy is literally beaten into submission by her husband,
representative of the patriarchy. The determinism in this
play is fully developed; Chrissy is a stubborn, optimistic
agent whose downfall is, nevertheless, inevitable considering
the strength of the opposition.

It is interesting to note, in light of the theme of wom-
en's solidarity discussed earlier, that Boom Boom Room
shows Chrissy reaching out to another woman, Susan, and to
a fellow victim of the patriarchy, Guy. Both of these attempts fail, however. Guy is no more willing to give up
the competition to be the most desirable object than Susan
is to give up her position of relative power to exploit within
the hierarchy. Thus, because this play rejects what feminist ideology would call the best hope of feminism, women's
support of one another, its deeply deterministic conclusion is
appropriate.

Wine in the Wilderness employs a similarly serious,
realistic style to reach far more optimistic conclusions.
Again, its seriousness adds to the directness of its impact
on an audience. This play is unique among those examined
in focusing on the relation between the demands black women
face in combating racism and those they face in combating
sexism.

It is often asserted that black women cannot oppose both, that in helping black men to assert the autonomy of blacks, they must continue to submit to oppression themselves as women. Wine in the Wilderness demonstrates simply and directly that this dilemma is only apparent. The clusters of associations in this play form a true ideal and a false one for black women. The false ideal is a glamorous but objectified and submissive black woman, supported by the threat of her opposite, the black matriarch, destroyer of black masculinity. The true ideal is represented in the agent, Tommy, who is supportive of her race, but who rejects the false ideal as well as the false threat of the black matriarchy to assert her own autonomy.

The simplicity and directness of Wine in the Wilderness are advantages in that they permit a clear rhetorical statement on a complex issue. Yet the easy resolution of the play may detract from its effect. The play is allied to the idealistic philosophy; simply by asserting herself, the agent easily triumphs over her oppressive situation. She does so, moreover, unaided by supportive women friends or by anyone else. The only other woman in the play, Cynthia, is the chief critic of Tommy's self-reliance.

It should be remembered, however, that the play, despite the obvious symbolism of the paintings, does not pretend to resolve the larger oppression of black women in society. Tommy has succeeded only in asserting her individual autonomy, achieving a personal transcendence of her oppression within a small circle of acquaintance. Through Bill's painting of her, she may inspire others to the same, personal transcendence. But there is no suggestion that Tommy has achieved a societal transformation simply by her own decision. Thus, the play is not completely unrealistic in its optimism, although it offers no more persuasive a resistance to the socio-sexual hierarchy than did The Bed Was Full or In the Boom Boom Room. Each of these plays depicts a solitary agent struggling unaided to achieve personal autonomy.

Birth and After Birth, in contrast, does not show an agent struggling for autonomy. Although it focuses on the nuclear family, a concern of contemporary women, and although it is authored by a woman, it does not share the pattern of symbolic action of the other plays. Hence, it cannot be considered feminist. In this play, the clusters of associations reveal two couples in opposition to each other, rather than woman in opposition to society. The couple that is oppressed by the limitations of the nuclear family, the Apples, does not struggle against this oppression. Instead, the Apples' action is to convert others to their own oppressive situation, first succeeding at converting their own son, and then failing to convert the opposing couple, the Freeds.

Because the Apples make no attempt to oppose their limiting environment, scene dominates agent in this play. Thus, it is allied to the materialistic philosophy. The play is deterministic in its conclusion, depicting an oppression so overwhelmingly effective that the Apples, despite their decaying condition, do not even perceive that they are oppressed.

Birth and After Birth, the only play examined that is not feminist in its rhetorical motive, shows less friendship and more competitiveness between women than do any of the other plays. In Boom Boom Room, Chrissy establishes a tenuous bond based on common experiences, which is later broken when Susan tries to exploit her sexually. In The Bed Was Full, Vera and Kali sometimes compete and sometimes cooperate with each other. At one point, Lewis makes Vera cry, and Kali leaps to her defense. Wine in the Wilderness shows an instant confidentiality and rapport established between Tommy and Cynthia. Although Cynthia recommends submissiveness to Tommy, her sympathies are with her rather than with Bill after only one brief conversation.

In Birth and After Birth, however, Sandy and Mia are complete opposites who never establish a common bond, however momentary. Instead, Sandy constantly compares herself unfavorably with Mia, and hopes to bring Mia down to her own low status. Birth and After Birth offers less hope of escape from society's oppression than any of the other plays examined, either by women's solidarity or by any other means.

Thus, like The Bed Was Full, Birth and After Birth is a farce without a truly comic ending. It closes with the establishment of an orderly society represented by the nuclear family, as a comedy should. But the nuclear family is not a new and more perfect order; it is an order which has been revealed as unjust, but which still controls the agents at the end. Moreover, the agents have not even opposed the unjust order in the course of the play.

The work of feminist theatre groups differs in several respects from the plays by individuals examined here. Most

obviously, this work differs in being more deliberately and
directly rhetorical. Four rhetorical strategies common to
much of this work have been described: sex-role reversal,
use of historical figures as role models, satire of traditional
sex roles, and direct portrayal of women's oppression. All
of these strategies are consistent with this study's definition
of feminist drama in their portrayal of an unjust socio-sexual
hierarchy. Many also show an agent opposing the hierarchy
and sometimes prevailing. However, these plays show two
characteristics unique to the work of groups. One is the use
of many protagonists rather than one in presentations united
by theme rather than by a through line of action. The second
is that many of these plays show women's achievement of autonomy through group solidarity, a theme that is conspicu-
ously absent from plays by most individual playwrights. For
Colored Girls represents an exception to this.

These differences cannot be attributed to a single
cause. The communal organization and the experimental
forms attempted by contemporary theatre groups, many of
them earlier than the feminist groups, have certainly been
an influence. However, the communal organization of feminist groups also reflects the feminist rejection of patriarchal
systems of authority. The emphasis on the experiences of
many women suggests the bonding that develops in feminist
consciousness-raising groups when women share their experiences of oppression. Finally, the emphasis on women's solidarity suggests the evolution of another phase in feminist ideology, yet to be absorbed by the larger culture.

Gerda Lerner suggests a model for the process of
women's emancipation from the male-defined world that emphasizes women's solidarity. In The Female Experience, already cited in the first chapter of this work, Lerner outlines
four phases in the process of women's emancipation. "The
first step toward emancipation is self-consciousness becoming aware of a distortion, a wrong: what women have been
taught about the world, what they see reflected in art, literature, philosophy, and religion is not quite appropriate to
them."[1] At this point, Lerner says, women, always perceived
as the "other" (to use de Beauvoir's phrase), begin to perceive man as the "other." This perception is the beginning
of feminist self-consciousness.

The second phase is a questioning of tradition. Often,
this is followed by tentative steps in new directions. The
third phase is "a reaching out toward other women, the slow,

painstaking search for sisterhood."[2] Only after women have
found each other does the fourth and final phase appear:

> Out of such communality and collectivity emerges
> feminist consciousness--a set of ideas which not
> only challenges patriarchal values and assumptions,
> but attempts to substitute for them a feminist sys-
> tem of ideas and values. This process of creating
> feminist consciousness has something, but by no
> means everything to do with the quest for women's
> rights, equality and justice--it has a great deal to
> do with the search for autonomy. [3]

Notice that the third phase, the "reaching out for other wom-
en," is central to the achievement of autonomy in Lerner's
theory.

Most plays examined individually in this study restrict
themselves to portraying the first two steps--the realization
of oppression and the rejection of existing tradition--in seeking the fourth step, woman's autonomy. The Bed Was Full,
In the Boom Boom Room, Wine in the Wilderness, and even
Birth and After Birth demonstrate a realization of women's
oppression in their portrayal of the unjust society. The three
plays that have been defined as feminist also show the agent
herself coming to this realization, and going on to question
existing traditions. Kali in The Bed Was Full rejects the
stereotypical sex roles reflecting traditional expectations of
women. Chrissy in Boom Boom Room questions the patriarchy's casting of her as the "other," asserting her own humanity. Tommy in Wine in the Wilderness rejects the traditional choices open to black women, matriarch or sex object,
and takes the "tentative steps in new directions" described by
Lerner in asserting herself to Bill.

None of these plays, however, shows the agent going
beyond her "tentative first steps" to achieve bonding with
other women. Wine in the Wilderness suggests that the agent
can achieve personal autonomy simply by her own decision,
without such bonding. The Bed Was Full and Boom Boom
Room indicate that realizing one's oppression and rejecting
tradition to move in new directions--unsupported by other
women--leads to violent reprisal and a return to the unjust
order. All of these plays, then, are either hopeful but simplistic in their conclusions, like Wine in the Wilderness, or
cognizant of the real difficulties and therefore despairing,
like Boom Boom Room. Only For Colored Girls and the

plays by feminist theatre groups offer bonding with other wom-
en as the means by which women may overcome their powerlessness as a group, and seek personal autonomy. Thus,
the plays written by groups are usually more advanced in the
feminist ideology they express.

        Those written by individuals, however, are far more
sophisticated in the rhetorical strategies they employ. As a
result, Burke's method of analyzing clusters of associations,
levels of significance, and patterns of action is of more value
in examining these plays than in examining the work of the
feminist theatre groups. In a play such as Boom Boom Room,
this kind of analysis can reveal the depth and complexity of
the play's depiction of sexist society. In The Bed Was Full,
focusing on the pattern of symbolic action can reveal an underlying rhetorical motive in what might have seemed a completely irrational farce. Even the plays by individuals, however, are sometimes so direct in their strategy as to demand
little of the depth of analysis possible in the Burkean method.

        It may be enlightening, for instance, to observe that
the image of Chrissy's father in Boom Boom Room operates
on all three of Burke's levels of significance, as her biologi-
cal father (familial), as representative of the patriarchy (abstract), and as physical threat of violence (sensory). It is
less of a revelation to observe that the paintings in Wine in
the Wilderness are not only, on the sensory level, paintings,
but are also, on the abstract level, representatives of the
painter's ideal of black womanhood. The painter himself says
that this is the case in the opening scene of the play. If the
feminist dramas written by individuals are often so direct as
to require little analysis, however, the plays written by feminist theatre groups frequently carry directness to a fault.

        In many of these group-written plays, there are no
levels of significance because the authors have chosen every
detail for its significance on the abstract level alone. Thus,
at one extreme are characters like the rapists in "Sexpot
Follies," abstractions who represent the evils of society, but
with less character development than the virtues and vices in
medieval morality plays. The more skillful of these plays,
such as RIFT's "Anne Hutchinson," offer some development
of character in images such as Anne's identification with her
garden, with its evocations of innocence and natural healing.
Even in this play, however, the hierarchy is represented by
the puppet ministers, one-dimensional abstractions. Nowhere
in these plays does one find the dark humor of The Bed Was

Full, in which Kali is offered a Band-Aid as a wedding ring, and is willing to accept it, or of Birth and After Birth, in which the housewife is dominated by a four-year-old who is literally six feet tall.   Nowhere in the plays by feminist theatre groups is the terrible compassion with which Chrissy in Boom Boom Room speaks of men: "They don't mean to hurt us....   They just don't know how not to." Although the plays by feminist theatre groups are more closely in touch with the evolution of feminist thought, they are far less so-phisticated than the plays by individuals in their rhetorical strategies.   As a result, they often fail to encompass the complexities of the situation they address.

     This failure to fully encompass complex situations may have several causes.   First and most obvious is the diffi-culty of creation by committee.   Among the plays produced by groups, those in which one person authors each independ-ent segment, or in which one person authors the whole on the approval of the group, are often the most controlled and unified.   When the author is already a professional playwright, as the members of the Westbeth collective were, the quality and control are generally even higher.   Plays that are the least unified and most simplistic, like "Lady in the Corner" and "Sexpot Follies," are generally the product of groups like Circle of the Witch, who are determinedly communal in everything they do, and who accept members without auditions or previous theatrical experience.

     A second cause for this lack of sophistication may be the relative youth both of the groups themselves and of the current wave of feminism in the U. S., which is barely ten years old.   A third, and more subtle cause may be the rela-tive relationships of feminist theatre groups and of individual authors to the feminist movement itself.   Feminist theatres are obviously more closely in touch with the evolution of femi-nist ideology than unaffiliated, individual authors are.   This is an advantage in making them cognizant of elements such as the significance of women's bonding.   On the other hand, such closeness to an ideology can also be a disadvantage. Authors who are devoted to a cause may have trouble depict-ing the ironies and ambivalence of the situations they show. Especially, they may be less likely to depict the enemies of a movement as complex figures who may present themselves as friends and family of the movement's members, or even as the thoughts of the members themselves.

     Feminist ideologists have widely recognized this last

danger, most often referred to as "the enemy in your head."
Diane Hope's dissertation, described in Chapter One, calls
the death of "traditional womanhood" a rhetorical goal of the
movement.[4] Movement rhetoric, however, is often the product of the group's observers, thinkers, and theorists. Feminist theatre, when it is the product of involved, active feminists, may not achieve the distance that such observers may,
or that individual authors not allied with the movement certainly can.

Finally, Hope's dissertation suggests a sense in which
the drama performed by feminist theatre groups may be less
rhetorically significant than the "drama" which the group's
members themselves undergo in their own lives. Hope suggests that the feminist movement, like other social movements,
articulates a rhetorical "drama of conflict" which reconstructs
reality for its participants. In the feminist movement, this
"drama of conflict" includes the isolation of participants and
the sharing of previously unshared cultural secrets.

Participation in the creation of feminist theatre may
involve the participants in both of the experiences described
by Hope. Members of a feminist theatre may feel that their
membership isolates them as a group from society. In creating their scripts, they draw upon previously unshared cultural secrets from their own experiences.[5] In this way,
members can enact a "drama of conflict" in their own lives.
Thus, the experience of participation in feminist theatre can
have a rhetorical impact on the group's members that is
quite distinct from the impact of its performances on an audience. The scripted performances of feminist theatre groups
may and often do lack rhetorical sophistication. But the
process of creating the scripts might, nevertheless, have
had a strong rhetorical impact on the group's members.

For Colored Girls comes closer than any of the other
plays examined to combining the feminist ideology of women's
solidarity with a high degree of rhetorical sophistication. In
For Colored Girls, fairly elaborate associational clusters form
a central opposition: the present unjust patriarchy opposing
the ideal, sororal and non-hierarchical community. The representatives of the patriarchy are not abstractions or villains
but the friends and lovers of the play's agents. The failure
of individuals' attempts to defy the patriarchy is depicted,
but is balanced by the positive power of women's community.
As a result, the play is more convincingly optimistic than
the others examined.

Because this optimistic resolution is largely on a spiritual plane, however, it may lack the directly social impact of Wine in the Wilderness or Boom Boom Room. Its fragmentary form also sacrifices the advantages of extended character development and continuously building action. Nevertheless, For Colored Girls is unique among the plays examined in being neither simplistic in its optimism nor despairing in its recognition of the complexity of oppression.

For Colored Girls also demonstrates most clearly the lack in the definition employed in this study, which posits a recognition of oppression, a rejection of tradition, and a search for autonomy, but without suggesting the means: women's support of one another. A definition that included this concept might, however, become restrictive as feminist ideology and feminist drama continue to develop. Already, it would exclude drama that simply reflects an earlier phase in the evolution of feminist thought. In its broad outlines, this definition has been a useful tool for the examination of the feminist impulse. The Burkean methodology, while it has not been taxed by the complexity of the material analyzed, has been theoretically appropriate to examining the rhetorical motive of an artistic form.

In the future, art will continue to reflect the progress of social movements in its rhetorical motives, as Burke has observed. If feminism continues to evolve, aspects of its ideology now familiar to only a few may become apparent to the larger society. When that happens, playwrights observant of society may create a drama without either the ideological or the artistic limitations of the drama examined here. A new form of feminist drama will then fully emerge that will artfully express the possibility of woman's autonomy.

Notes

1. Gerda Lerner, The Female Experience (Indianapolis: Bobbs-Merrill Company, Inc., 1977), p. xxiii.

2. Ibid., p. xxiv.

3. Ibid.

4. Diane S. Hope, "A Rhetorical Definition of Movements: The Drama of Rebirth in Radical Feminism" (Ph.D. dissertation, State University of New York at Buffalo, 1975).

5. Hope's "previously unshared cultural experiences" are
    the personal histories of women in consciousness-
    raising groups, who legitimize their lives by sharing
    their own histories. Feminist theatre groups experi-
    ence this kind of sharing, as well as a rediscovery
    and sharing of women's history in the larger sense.
    Additionally, members of feminist theatre groups may
    share the creation of an alternate, feminist view of
    the culture, transcending the patriarchal view.

SELECTED BIBLIOGRAPHY

Primary Materials

A. Published

Childress, Alice. Wine in the Wilderness. In Plays By and About Women, pp. 379-421. Edited by Victoria Sullivan and James Hatch. New York: Random House, 1974.

Drexler, Rosalyn. The Line of Least Existence and Other Plays. Introduction by Richard Gilman. New York: Random House, 1967.

Howe, Tina. Birth and After Birth. In The New Women's Theatre: Ten Plays by Contemporary American Women, pp. 99-188. Edited by Honor Moore. New York: Random House, 1977.

Lamb, Myrna. The Mod Donna and Scyklon Z: Plays of Women's Liberation. New York: Pathfinder Press, 1971.

Rabe, David. In the Boom Boom Room. New York: Alfred A. Knopf, 1974.

Rhode Island Feminist Theatre. The Johnnie Show. Shubert Playbook Series, vol. 4, no. 2.

_____. Persephone's Return. Shubert Playbook Series, vol. 3, no. 2.

_____. Taking It Off. Providence: Hellcoal Press, 1973.

Shepard, Andrea. "Day Upon Day." The Second Wave, Summer 1974, pp. 28-37.

B. Unpublished

Aaron, Joyce and Tarlo, Luna. "Acrobatics," 1975. Per-
    formed by Boulder Feminist Theatre.

Boulder Feminist Theatre Collective. 2043 Pine Street,
    Boulder, Colorado 80302. Publicity brochures and
    press clippings printed in 1976-1978 or undated.

Circle of the Witch. 2953 Bloomington So., Minneapolis,
    Minnesota 55407. Programs, publicity brochures,
    and newsletters printed in 1977 and 1978 or undated.

Circle of the Witch. "Sexpot Follies: A Satire on Sexism
    from Our Own Lives and Experiences," June 1974.

_____. "Lady in the Corner," copyright pending 1975.

Ferguson, Cynthia A. Circle of the Witch, Minneapolis,
    Minnesota. Interview, taped in response to written
    questions, November 1977.

Leavitt, Dinah. Boulder Feminist Theatre, Boulder, Colo-
    rado. Interview, August 1977.

McAllister, Ada. Rhode Island Feminist Theatre, Providence,
    Rhode Island. Interview in Columbia, Missouri, No-
    vember 1977.

Rhode Island Feminist Theatre. Box 9083, Providence, Rhode
    Island 02940. Programs, publicity brochures, and
    press clippings, printed in 1977 and 1978 or undated.

_____. "Anne Hutchinson: Rhode Island's First Independ-
    ent Woman." Adapted to video by Brandon French and
    Ada McAllister, 1977.

_____. "O Women's Piece," n. d.

Sarver, Judy. B & O Theatre, Champaign, Illinois. Inter-
    view in Columbia, Missouri, November 1977.

Walker, Dolores. Westbeth Feminist Playwrights Collective,
    New York, New York. Interview, December 1975.

Westbeth Playwrights' Feminist Collective. Publicity flyers
    and press clippings, printed in 1973, 1975 or undated.

_____. Unpublished review material, short skits by Gwendolyn Gunn, Pat Horan, Linda Kline, Chryse Maile, Sally Ordway, and A. Piotrowski.

Theory and Criticism

A. Books

Adams, Elsie and Briscoe, Mary Louise, ed. Up Against the Wall, Mother ... On Women's Liberation. California: Macmillan & Sons, 1974.

Allen, Mary, The Necessary Blankness: Women in Major American Fiction of the Sixties. Bloomington: Indiana University Press, 1976.

Auchincloss, Louis. Pioneers and Caretakers: A Study of Nine American Women Novelists. Minneapolis: University of Minnesota Press, 1965.

Beauvoir, Simone de. The Second Sex. Translated by H. M. Parshley. New York: Alfred A. Knopf, 1970.

Borden, Karen W. and Rinns, Fauneil J. Feminist Literary Criticism: A Symposium. San Jose: Diotima Press, 1974.

Burke, Kenneth. A Grammar of Motives and a Rhetoric of Motives. Cleveland: World Publishing Co., 1972.

_____. The Philosophy of Literary Form. Baton Rouge: Louisiana University Press, 1967. Paperback ed., New York: Vintage Books, 1957-61.

_____. The Rhetoric of Religion. Boston: Beacon Press, 1961.

Daly, Mary. Beyond God the Father: Toward a Philosophy of Women's Liberation. Boston: Beacon Press, 1973.

Donovan, Josephine, ed. Feminist Literary Criticism: Explorations in Theory. Louisville: University of Kentucky Press, 1975.

Goulianos, Joan. By a Woman Writt: Literature from Six Centuries by and about Women. New York: Penguin Books, 1974.

150   Feminist Drama

Hartnoll, Phyllis, ed. The Concise Oxford Companion to the
    Theatre. London: Oxford University Press, 1972.

Heilbrun, Carolyn G. Toward a Recognition of Androgyny.
    New York: Alfred A. Knopf, 1973.

Hess, Thomas B. and Baker, Elizabeth C. Art and Sexual
    Politics. New York: Collier Books, 1971.

Johnson, Wendell Stacy. Sex and Marriage in Victorian
    Poetry. Ithaca: Cornell University Press, 1975.

Juhasz, Suzanne. Naked and Fiery Forms: Modern Ameri-
    can Poetry by Women, A New Tradition. New York:
    Harper Colophon Books, 1976.

Lakoff, Robin. Language and Woman's Place. New York:
    Harper Colophon Books, 1975.

Lerner, Gerda. The Female Experience. Indianapolis:
    Bobbs-Merrill Company, Inc., 1977.

Martin, Wendy. The American Sisterhood. New York: Har-
    per & Row, 1972.

Millett, Kate. Sexual Politics. Garden City: Doubleday,
    1970.

Moers, Ellen. Literary Women. New York: Doubleday, 1976.

Morgan, Ellen. "Humanbecoming: Form and Focus in the Neo-
    Feminist Novel." In Images of Women in Fiction:
    Feminist Perspectives, pp. 180-204. Edited by Susan
    Koppelman Cornillon. Bowling Green: Bowling Green
    University Popular Press, 1972.

Rogers, Katherine M. The Troublesome Helpmate: A His-
    tory of Misogyny in Literature. Seattle: University
    of Washington Press, 1966.

Rueckert, William H., ed. Critical Responses to Kenneth
    Burke. Minneapolis: University of Minnesota Press,
    1969.

_____. Kenneth Burke and the Drama of Human Relations.
    Minneapolis: University of Minnesota Press, 1963.

Russ, Joanna. "What Can a Heroine Do?" In Images of
    Women in Fiction: Feminist Perspectives, pp. 4-15.
    Edited by Susan Koppelman Cornillon. Bowling Green:
    Bowling Green University Popular Press, 1972.

Sainer, Arthur. "Rosalyn Drexler." In Contemporary Dram-
    atists, pp. 208-209. Edited by James Vinson. New
    York: St. James Press, 1973.

Sanborn, Sara. Review of The Cosmopolitan Girl. New
    York Times, 30 March 1975, sec. 7, p. 5.

Spacks, Patricia Meyer. The Female Imagination. New York:
    Alfred A. Knopf, 1975.

Warren, Barbara. The Feminine Image in Literature. Ro-
    chelle Park: Hayden Book Co. Inc., 1973.

Yates, Gayle Graham. What Women Want: The Ideas of the
    Movement. Cambridge, Massachusetts: Harvard Uni-
    versity Press, 1975.

B. Articles

Anonymous. Review of In the Boom Boom Room. New York
    Times, 5 December, 1974, p. 55.

Bammer, Angelika. "Toward a Feminist-Marxist Criticism."
    WCML Workshop in Feminist Criticism, Midwest Mod-
    ern Language Association Convention, 1976. (Type-
    written.)

Barnes, Clive. Review of Apple Pie by Myrna Lamb. New
    York Times, 13 February 1976, p. 18.

Beal, Frances M. "Double Jeopardy: To Be Black and Fe-
    male." In Sisterhood Is Powerful, pp. 340-353. Edited
    by Robin Morgan. New York: Random House, 1970.

Beck, Evelyn T. and Lanser, Susan S. "Feminist Criticism:
    A Methodology of One's Own?" WCML Workshop in
    Feminist Criticism, Midwest Modern Language Asso-
    ciation Convention, 1976. (Typewritten.)

Campbell, Karlyn Kohrs. "The Rhetoric of Women's Libera-
    tion: An Oxymoron." Quarterly Journal of Speech 59
    (February 1973): 74-86.

Christ, Carol P. "Margaret Atwood: The Surfacing of Women's Spiritual Quest and Vision." Signs 2 (Winter 1976): 316-330.

Didion, Joan. Why I Write. From a Regents' Lecture at the University of California at Berkeley, n. d.

Drexler, Rosalyn. "The New Androgyny." Vogue, February 1977, p. 94.

Dunbar, Roxanne. "Female Liberation as the Basis for Social Revolution." In Sisterhood Is Powerful, pp. 477-492. Edited by Robin Morgan. New York: Random House, 1970.

Ehrenreich, Barbara. "Toward Socialist Feminism." Heresies, January 1977, pp. 4-7.

Hope, Diane S. "Redefinition of Self: A Comparison of the Rhetoric of the Women's Liberation and Black Liberation Movements." Today's Speech 23 (Winter 1975): 17-25.

Kauffmann, Stanley. "Stanley Kauffmann on Theater." New Republic, December 1, 1973, p. 22.

Kaufman, Michael W. "The Delicate World of Reprobation: A Note on the Black Revolutionary Theatre." Educational Theatre Journal 23 (December 1971): 446-459.

Kennedy, Florynce. "Institutionalized Oppression vs. the Female." In Sisterhood Is Powerful, pp. 438-446. Edited by Robin Morgan. New York: Random House, 1970.

Kerr, Walter. "David Rabe's 'House' Is Not a Home." New York Times, 2 May 1976, sec. 2, p. 5.

Kolodny, Annette. "Literary Criticism." Signs 2 (Winter 1976): 404-421.

_____. "Some Notes on Defining a 'Feminist Literary Criticism.'" Journal of Critical Inquiry 2 (Autumn 1975): 75-92.

Lamb, Margaret. "Feminist Criticism." The Drama Review 18 (September 1974): 46-50.

Oliver, Edith. Review of Apple Pie by Myrna Lamb. New
    Yorker, 23 February 1976, p. 82.

Peslikis, Irene. "Resistances to Consciousness." In Sister-
    hood Is Powerful, pp. 337-339. Edited by Robin
    Morgan. New York: Random House, 1970.

Peters, Margot. "Traditional and Feminist Historical-Bio-
    graphical Criticism." WCML Workshop in Feminist
    Criticism, Midwest Modern Language Association Con-
    vention, 1976. (Typewritten.)

Pratt, Annis. "Archetypal Theory and Women's Fiction:
    1688-1975." WCML Panel: "The Theory of Feminist
    Literary Critics," Midwest Modern Language Associa-
    tion Convention, 1975. (Typewritten.)

_____. "The New Feminist Criticism." College English
    32 (May 1971): 872-878.

Regelson, Regina. Review of New Feminist Repertory. New
    York Times, 18 May 1969, sec. 2, p. 1.

Riach, W. A. D. "Telling It Like It Is: An Examination of
    Black Theatre As Rhetoric." Quarterly Journal of
    Speech 56 (April 1970): 179-186.

Rich, Adrienne. "When We Dead Awaken: Writing as Re-
    vision." College English 34 (October 1972): 179-186.

Rosenwasser, Marie J. "Rhetoric and the Progress of the
    Women's Liberation Movement." Today's Speech 20
    (Summer 1972): 45-56.

Shank, Theodore. "Political Theatre as Popular Entertain-
    ment: The San Francisco Mime Troupe." The Drama
    Review (March 1974): 110-117.

Showalter, Elaine. "Literary Criticism." Signs 1 (Winter
    1975): 461-486.

Sproat, Kezia Vanmeter. "Formalism and the Feminist
    Correction." WCML Workshop in Feminist Criticism,
    Midwest Modern Language Association Convention,
    1976. (Typewritten.)

Staton, Shirley. "Psychology Instructs the Female Critic."

WCML Workshop in Feminist Criticism, Midwest Modern Language Association Convention, 1976. (Type-
written.)

Watson, Barbara Bellow. "On Power and the Literary Text."
Signs 1 (August 1975): 111-118.

Williams, Maxine. "Why Women's Liberation Is Important
to Black Women." The Militant, 3 July 1970; reprint
ed. in Black Women's Liberation, pp. 3-11. New
York: Pathfinder Press, 1970.

History

A. Books

Childress, Alice, ed. Black Scenes. New York: Doubleday
and Company, 1971.

Filene, Peter Gabriel. Him/Her/Self: Sex Roles in Modern
America. New York: New American Library, 1974.

Goulianos, Joan. "Women and the Avant-Garde Theater."
In Woman: An Issue, pp. 257-267. Edited by Lee R.
Edwards, Mary Heath and Lisa Baskin. Boston: Little
Brown & Co., 1972.

Himelstein, Morgan Y. Drama Was a Weapon: The Left-
Wing Theatre in New York 1929-1941. New Bruns-
wick, N. J.: Rutgers University Press, 1963.

Hole, Judith and Levine, Ellen. Rebirth of Feminism. New
York: Quadrangle Books, 1971.

Kraditor, Alison S. Up from the Pedestal: Selected Writings
in the History of American Feminism. Chicago: Quadrangle Books, 1968.

O'Neill, William L., ed. The American Sexual Dilemma.
New York: Holt, Rinehart & Winston, 1972.

Rabe, David. The Basic Training of Pavlo Hummel and
Sticks and Bones. Introduction by David Rabe. New
York: Viking Press, 1973.

Rabkin, Gerald. Drama and Commitment: Politics in the Ameri-

can Theatre of the Thirties. Bloomington: Indiana
University Press, 1964.

Smiley, Sam. The Drama of Attack: Didactic Plays of the
American Depression. Columbia: University of Missouri Press, 1972.

Sochen, June, ed. The New Feminism in Twentieth-Century
America. Lexington: D. C. Heath and Co., 1971.

Taylor, Karen Malpede. People's Theatre in Amerika. New
York: Drama Book Specialists/Publishers, 1972.

B. Articles

Childress, Alice. Interview in New York Times, 2 February 1969, sec. 2, p. 1.

dell' Olio, Anselma. "The Founding of the New Feminist
Theatre," pp. 101-102. In Notes from the Second
Year: Women's Liberation--Major Writings of the
Radical Feminists, April, 1970.

Drexler, Rosalyn. Interview in New York Times, 20 May
1973, sec. 2, p. 1.

Gillespie, Patti. "A Listing of Feminist Theatres." Theatre News 10 (November 1977): 22-24.

Gottlieb, Lois C. "The Double Standard Debate in Early
Twentieth-Century American Drama." Michigan
Academician 7 (Spring 1975): 441-451.

_____. "The Perils of Freedom: The New Woman in
Three American Plays of the 1900's." Canadian Review of American Studies 6 (1975): 84-98.

Johnston, Laurie. "Sexism in the Theatre Can Be a Boon."
New York Times, 6 February 1973, p. 26.

Lazier, Gil. "Obituary for a Gentle Agit-Prop Play." Educational Theatre Journal 23 (May 1971): 135-151.

Rea, Charlotte. "The New York Feminist Theatre Troupe."
The Drama Review 18 (September 1974): 132-133.

_____. "Women for Women." The Drama Review 18 (December 1974): 77-87.

_____. "Women's Theatre Groups." The Drama Review 16 (June 1972): 79-89.

Rabe, David. Interview in New York Times, 24 November 1973, p. 22.

_____. Interview in New York Times, 25 April 1976, sec. 2, p. 12.

_____. Interview in New York Times, 12 May 1976, p. 34.

Dissertations

Hope, Diane S. "A Rhetorical Definition of Movements: The Drama of Rebirth in Radical Feminism." Ph. D. dissertation, State University of New York at Buffalo, 1975.

Wagner, Phyllis Jane. "Megan Terry: Political Playwright." Ph. D. dissertation, University of Denver, 1975.

Zastrow, Silvia Virginia Horning. "The Structure of Selected Plays by American Women Playwrights: 1920-1970." Ph. D. dissertation, Northwestern University, 1975.

INDEX